THE DECORATION OF ENGLISH PORCELAIN

ALSO BY STANLEY W. FISHER

English Blue-and-White Porcelain
of the Eighteenth Century

SPODE VASE: about 1820

The Decoration of
English Porcelain

A Description of the
Painting and Printing on English Porcelain
of the Period 1750 to 1850

STANLEY W. FISHER

DEREK VERSCHOYLE
14 CARLISLE STREET, SOHO SQUARE, LONDON WI

First published in 1954 by
DEREK VERSCHOYLE LIMITED
14 Carlisle Street, Soho Square, London, W1

Printed in Great Britain by
HUNT, BARNARD AND CO LTD
AYLESBURY

TO ANTHONY AND PAUL

CONTENTS

PREFACE

The modern porcelain collector has at his disposal an extremely large range of reference books, and because of the rapid rate at which knowledge has accumulated, more and more specialist monographs are being written. We live in an age of specialization, in antiques as in all else, and the serious collector of ceramics gathers together a representative display of pieces of a particular provenance, period, or style, in preference to a more catholic one which may well be equally beautiful but which can never approach anything like finality. Such a collection has other advantages, for the specialist becomes expert in a particular sort of ware, his collection is mentally more satisfying, and the search for specimens is infinitely more difficult and consequently more engrossing. He has replaced, by and large, the collector of the old school, who surrounded himself with pottery and porcelain simply because he loved it for its beauty, and who knew little, and often cared less, about its history, its composition, or its possible rarity.

This book may be, I hope, a new sort of reference book, which may be acceptable to collectors of either class, to the casual and to the finical alike, because it deals with a criterion of assessment which must be acceptable to both – Decoration. By whatever standards a piece of porcelain is judged, and whatever its intrinsic value, the final verdict must always depend on the decoration upon it. Naturally enough, there is such a thing as beauty of form, of pleasing proportions and balance, which needs no additional ornament, and because of this it has long been accepted that decoration of any kind should always enhance but should never detract – that the wood must never be hidden by the trees. Nevertheless, there may be exceptions to the most desirable and well-founded of rules, and changing taste, supported by improved technical achievement, has on occasion led to the transfer of emphasis from the porcelain to the painting upon it. Vulgarity, ostentation, over-decoration, are all epithets which have been used to describe painting which draws attention and which holds it to the exclusion of all else, but there is surely another side to the question. 'I know I ought not to like it, but I am afraid I do,' said someone who resented 'education' in art, and if there are those whose interest lies more in the study of skilled brushwork, magnificent colours, and intricate gilding than in the appreciation of a lovely paste and glaze, then their plaint is excuse enough. There is beauty in all ceramic decoration, though it appears in many a different guise.

As the title implies, I have confined myself to the decoration found only on English porcelain – my Welsh readers will perhaps forgive me if for convenience sake I quite wrongly include the Nantgarw and Swansea wares under that heading. The styles of decoration on pottery and porcelain do sometimes run on parallel lines, but a description of the many dissimilarities would entail a volume too bulky to contemplate, and for the same reason all but incidental description of foreign wares must be omitted. In the latter regard I have fewer regrets, because there is hardly any Oriental or Continental style which cannot be found on our native productions, either copied exactly, as in later days, or charmingly anglicized by the pioneers.

It is sometimes difficult to appreciate the conditions under which the early decorators had to work, conditions which were often such as to make us wonder at the hard-won skill and perseverance which were responsible for the beauty which we admire to-day. The way of the pioneer porcelain maker was indeed hard, and it is perhaps a good thing at this point for us to try to look back for a moment at the nature of the English porcelain factory of the early 1750s, at its organization and at its problems.

Naturally enough, the potters already skilled in the making of earthenware or delft had great advantages when they began to make the finer, translucent porcelain; they possessed potting skill and proved equipment. At the other extreme were the enthusiastic amateurs, such as Dr Johnson, who we are told experimented with eggshells and gum. Then there were men such as Sprimont of Chelsea, Frye of Bow, and Wall and Davis of Worcester, who began with some sort of workable formula, and who were able to raise the capital necessary either to build a pottery or to take over the equipment of one already existing. Whatever the beginnings, there is no doubt that the initial difficulty lay in the making of porcelain rather than in its decoration. Kiln losses were enormous, and we can see from surviving specimens that warped and even cracked pieces were considered worthy of being painted and sold.

Behind the potter, as often as not, was a patron. In the East the Emperor was the virtual owner of the potteries and the potters, and on the Continent Royalty dictated the taste and footed the bill. In this country however the whims of private individuals often decided the fate of the first factories, particularly at the turn of the century, when perfected pastes made possible the splendidly painted pieces which enhanced their mansions or which served as worthy presents to their friends and Royal masters. Thus, at Rockingham, Earl Fitzwilliam's subsidy staved off disaster for a few years, and the finest Swansea porcelain owed its manufacture to Lewis Weston Dillwyn, who was tempted by the beauty of Billingsley's paste to make it at a ruinous loss. Without patrons, only the large potteries could hope to survive, and while Worcester and Derby have continued almost uninterrupted to the present day there was a constant stream of failures. Some potteries, such as those of Longton Hall and Lowestoft, simply closed down, while others were amalgamated with larger concerns.

In this struggle for existence what was the position of the decorator? It is obvious that he must have been a man with previous experience, either in the painting of earthenware or in enamelling establishments such as those at Battersea or Bilston. There was probably no lack of painters of a sort, in the Potteries, at Liverpool, or at Bristol, who knew the technique of colour mixing and firing, however unsuited were their styles to the new ware. From these districts and, as we shall see, from the Continental factories, artists were attracted to the centres of porcelain making, though frequent and urgent advertisements tend to indicate that there was a scarcity of those whose brushwork was sufficiently delicate. It was necessary for such delicacy to go hand in hand with versatility, and with an inventiveness which at times produced designs which owed nothing to any foreign source.

There are several reasons why collectors of old English porcelain can seldom safely identify a specimen on the evidence of decoration alone. Most of the early motifs and patterns were copied from the same foreign originals. Original designs of one of our own factories would be copied by others if they proved acceptable to the popular taste. Artists wandered from one factory to another, taking their ideas with them, and skilled ones found it profitable to employ others to paint either upon ware which they bought 'in the white' or upon similar ware sent to them by one or other of the factories or china dealers.

Artists working inside the factory decorating shops were of two kinds. Some of the work was purely repetitive, especially when it was done in underglaze blue, and we can guess that it was poorly paid. It is said that at Lowestoft such work was done by girls, and at Worcester the same simple pattern may be accompanied by a multitude of different artists' marks. But the more elaborate designs, even of the early days, called for more skilled treatment, as for example the gem-like 'chinoiseries' once ascribed to Michael Edkins of Bristol, and the crowded but wonderfully colourful 'mandarin' patterns of polychrome Liverpool. Later on, in the first quarter of the 19th century, we find the masterpieces of flower, bird, landscape, and figure painting described in later chapters, and the intricate, accurately drawn gilding usually found upon them. Their authors were men such as Peg the Quaker, Billingsley, and Baxter, who were never content to remain for long in one place, and who sometimes stopped work for long periods owing to fits of drunkenness or religious scruple. Many of them were renowned in other spheres, as drawing masters, illustrators, engravers, portrait painters, or miniaturists. As for the decorating establishments, it can be said that 'London decoration' vies with the best of the factory work. Many a fine piece of Bow or Chelsea was finished at Mr Giles's studios, and at a later date even the wealthy Chamberlains or Flights did not scorn to send their finest wares to be painted elsewhere.

Little mention has been made in the following chapters of factory history or technical peculiarity, since I am concerned predominantly with aesthetic values. I have tried to deal faithfully with the origins, development, and merits of the many different styles of painted and printed ornament which are found on English porcelain during the first 100 years of its manufacture, in chronological order where possible, and I have completely omitted figures as being outside the scope of this book. The illustrations are chosen from many hundreds which have been made available to me, and I take this opportunity of thanking all those who have helped me in this regard – those who have allowed me to photograph their treasures, those whose photographs I have used, and those whose I have reluctantly put aside. Their names are too numerous to mention here. In addition I would thank my publisher, Mr Derek Verschoyle, for his invaluable encouragement and guidance, and Mr Gresham Copeland, for his technical help and for the many facilities placed at my disposal.

S. W. F.

Bewdley
Worcestershire

THE DECORATION OF ENGLISH PORCELAIN

CHAPTER ONE

The Nature of Coloured Decoration

The urge to decorate his ware must have been felt by the most primitive potter, or indeed perhaps more by him than by his more sophisticated successors. Even in pre-historic times there were colours in plenty, of a sort, the organic pigments with which native peoples painted their shields, basketry, gourds, or even their bodies, but they were useless to the potter because they were destroyed by heat. Later, when man made porcelain, even greater heat was necessary, up to 1400 degrees centigrade for the Oriental, higher still for the Continental, and well over 1000 for the fritt and bone bodies of our own country. Naturally enough, there has been a steady discovery of new pigments through the centuries, and the re-discovery of many which were known to the Chinese, but of which the secret had for long been lost. New metals have been identified, such as platinum, chromium, uranium, titanium, and antimony, whose salts have given new colours. Such chemists' work, and the improvements of the engineer, have all contributed to the greater expansion of the decorator's palette, and to the ways in which it may be used.

Coloured decoration may be applied to porcelain in several different ways. A body (or paste) may itself be coloured, in the manner of the Wedgwood 'jaspers', of the well-known lavender Rockingham cottages, and of the 'cane-ware' made famous by Ridgway, but coloured porcelain bodies have never been in favour, and we pass on to the second method, the application of coloured glazes. This is responsible for some of the finest and rarest of Oriental porcelains, the famous 'monochromes' which are to be found at their earliest among the Sung wares of 800 years ago. As we have already hinted, the pigments had to be metallic ones, such as the oxides of iron and copper which were the first to be used, and which gave a surprisingly large range of colours, depending on the composition of the glaze and the temperature of the kiln. Most cele-brated are the greenish 'celadons', but there were also innumerable greys, browns, and even purple. Later, other metallic salts were used, such as those of manganese (which gave brighter purples or, with iron oxide, the lustrous 'mirror black'), of cobalt, lead, and copper. The Chinese porcelain was a 'true' one, made of china-clay and china-stone, calling for the highest firing temperature, and a glaze which fused at a lower heat had to be applied to the fired biscuit body, after which the whole was refired.

I

Even then its fluid character in the kiln made it unsuitable for brushwork, with the result that we have this inheritance of truly magnificent pieces whose only decoration is their shimmering glaze. This is not a description of Chinese wares, but it may be of interest to mention a few of the many varieties – peach-bloom, tea-dust, iron-rust, *sang-de-boeuf*, apple-green, and kingfisher-blue. In this country coloured glazes have been used mainly on earthenware, resulting in such lovely wares as those of Astbury, Whieldon, and the Woods, the revivals of William de Morgan and 'Ruskin' pottery, and the utilitarian and much-copied brown-glazed Rockingham; only very occasionally are they seen on porcelain, as, for example, on the rare mottled-brown and gilded specimens of the latter factory.

It is clear that the fewer firings a piece of porcelain has to undergo, the more cheaply and quickly can it be produced. For this reason alone, apart from the additional firing risks, colours which can be applied to the body before it is glazed possess great advantages. Unfortunately, these underglaze colours, as they are called, have until recent times been comparatively few in number – the Chinese had only two which would safely stand the heat of the glazing kiln. Of these the more important by far was blue, produced from cobalt oxide in varying degrees of purity, a blue which was known to the Persians at an even earlier date. Enormous use was made of its possibilities on the Oriental 'blue-and-white' wares which flooded Europe during the 17th and 18th centuries, and the best specimens are incomparably lovely, with the 'Mohammedan Blue', as it was called, applied in graded washes to boldly drawn, economical outline. 'Blue as a sapphire' and 'blue as the sky after rain' were two of the Chinese descriptions which are perhaps most expressive. The pieces which became available to the Continental factories at such places as Florence, St Cloud, Chantilly, and Berlin were not usually of the highest standards, but very occasionally we find a specimen, either from the Continent or from one of our own early fritt-paste factories, which is clearly a copy of the rare and true K'hang H'si (1622–1722) or Yung Cheng (1722–55), though even pieces from these accomplished periods are held inferior, in China, to the bolder and more freely drawn 15th-century ones.

An almost unlimited range of tone is obtainable from the cobalt oxide, depending upon its purity. The purest oxide gives the brightest blue, which is the reason why so much early English 'blue-and-white' ranges from dark indigo to violet in colour. Impurity gives to the early pieces an indefinable charm which is lacking in modern ones; manganese in very small quantities gives the purplish hue which can be seen on the Caughley porcelain of the 1790s, or, in larger proportions, the slatey-grey tone which is evident on a great deal of Worcester.

The other Chinese underglaze colour, used often with enamels, was a deep blood-red evolved from copper, and this too was imitated by European decorators, though with less success. On the other hand, they introduced new ones, notably a very rich opaque green from oxide of chromium, which was in use at Meissen during the first quarter of the 19th century; a wide range of greens could be produced by mixing the cobalt and chromium salts in varying proportions, while those of chromium and iron gave pleasing browns. In the same way, blacks and greys were possible if salts of copper, iron, and cobalt were mixed together. An examination of modern coloured wares will naturally show that great strides have been and are still being made in the invention of new underglaze colours to keep pace with the ever-increasing use of transfer printing.

Overglaze colours, or enamels, are derived from the same metallic oxides, but because they are fired in a 'muffle' kiln at a comparatively low temperature (about 700 degrees centigrade) their range was considerable even in the early days of Oriental porcelain making. An enamel is simply a mineral salt either mixed with some sort of glass in powder form, or else fused together with it, finely ground, and applied with suitable mediums. Thus, nowadays, turpentine is used to mix the colour, and fat oil to stiffen it to a workable consistency. Masters as they were of enamel pigments the Chinese were not always the first in the field, as witness their porcelain painted in 'famille rose' style; gold, in the form of 'Purple of Cassius', can give practically every shade of red, from pale pink to purple, but its secret reached China from Europe, and not until about 1720 were the K'hang H'si artists able to make use of it, a curious reversal of the usual trend of discovery.

Although enamels are applied over the glaze, their appearance is not the same on every kind of porcelain. On the 'true' paste of the Oriental, of the Continental, and of the few English factories which made it, on which the glaze had a high melting point, they remained encrusted on the surface, whereas they sank into the 'softer' glazes of an artificial porcelain. Indeed, it was the custom at the Sèvres factory to apply a coating of a softer glaze to reserved panels intended for enamel decoration, in order to obtain this more mellow appearance. In addition to the ordinary use of enamels we should not forget the 'émaillé sur biscuit' of the Chinese, in which no glaze was used at all, the enamels being so arranged as to cover the entire surface of the biscuit body, thus giving remarkably soft colouring. In later times yet another sort of enamel was made at Sèvres and at Mintons, in the 19th century, where the colours were mixed with 'slip' and applied in washes to build up a relief decoration known as 'pâte sur pâte' [112].

Broadly speaking, then, we have the four classes of decoration – coloured paste, coloured glazes, underglaze colours, and enamels, and the decorative styles in which they were used will be discussed more fully in later pages. In the meantime there is yet another different sort of decoration which must not be forgotten, the use of gilding, the application of real gold by one of several means. Gilding of any sort is uncommon on early Chinese porcelain, probably because its makers revered their ware as something precious in itself, and were unwilling to gild the lily. On the other hand, the art has always been practised in Europe, and gold is found a great deal in conjunction with coloured decoration, or by itself.

Lustred surfaces do not properly come within the scope of this book, since they are almost entirely confined to earthenware. Nevertheless, certain classes of early 19th-century porcelain, such as New Hall and Liverpool, have silver borders or are decorated with slight foliate patterns in silver or pink lustre. The original use of lustre was to imitate the appearance of vessels of gold, silver, or copper, and to this end salts of copper, gold, and platinum were used to produce thin metallic layers upon the ware. Copper was used to give effects of gold, bronze, or copper, platinum gave silver, and gold gave various shades of pink. Lustre was used not only to cover an entire piece, but also to provide a background to painted or printed decoration, while the rarer 'resist' lustre was produced by masking selected patterned parts of the surface with a soluble pigment which could be washed away after the whole had been lustred. Lustre as we know it is of comparatively late date, though of course an earlier use of it is to be seen on some of the Hispano-Moresque tin-glazed wares of the 16th century.

There are three main methods of applying these various classes of colour. Painting with a brush gives greatest scope for freedom and virility of expression, and 'hand-painted' has always been regarded as the hall-mark of decoration in any sort of craft. Secondly, there is the blowing of a powdered pigment through a tube, closed at one end with gauze, against a sized surface, giving in effect an underglaze ground-colour known as 'powder-blue', the 'soufflé' blue of the Chinese. The peculiar granulated surface thus produced was used to good effect by the decorators of Worcester,[1] Lowestoft, Bow, and Caughley. Lastly, the various ways of transfer printing, for the invention of which many claims have been put forward. Certainly, printing was done on enamels at Battersea and Bilston, at Liverpool by Sadler and Green, at Worcester, and even at Bow, but there is no absolute certainty about its original introduction, and we are on surer ground in saying that by 1757 Robert Hancock's engraved patterns were in use at Worcester. The process is familiar enough, line engravings were made on copper plates, from which the pigment was transferred to paper and thence to the ware. At first the printing was overglaze, chiefly in black (and looking remarkably like the black enamel drawings on Chinese porcelain) but also in lilac and red. Outside

[1]Frank Lloyd Collection, pl 2, no 5.

decorators such as Giles used the printed porcelain for additional decoration in enamels, applied sparingly so as not to obscure the close shading and cross-hatching of the engraving. Then, within a few years, followed printing in underglaze blue, which called for a different style of engraving, but which provided a most welcome 'bread and butter' line for certain factories, notably those at Worcester, Caughley, Lowestoft, and Liverpool. There was naturally a great demand for a cheap ware which was so like the Chinese 'Blue Nankin'. Towards the end of the century a new technique was developed, in which a stippled print was applied to the ware from a 'bat' or sheet of glue, instead of paper. Oil was used instead of colour, and powdered colour dusted on to the transferred oiled design. Bat printing was soon in universal use, for it was well suited to the reproduction of the classical Bartolozzi and Kauffmann subjects which were then popular. It was adopted by such famous concerns as Spode and Minton, and it has never been entirely superseded. With the advent of blue-printing the original line-engraved prints went out of favour, and the overglaze process was retained mainly for the quick transferring of outlines, to be filled in with enamel washes. This device is still used, though for domestic wares underglaze printing in colour is both quicker and cheaper. Most of the improvements in this regard took place early in the 19th century, when it would appear that two colour makers named Booth and Twigg introduced their 'gaudy colours'. A bright pink was one of the earliest, to be followed by brown, green, orange, yellow, black, purple, and many others. At first each colour was applied separately, but the invention of lithography made possible the colour transfer as we now understand it. However much we may dislike the short cut to decoration, it cannot be denied that it has brought well-designed wares within the reach of all.

CHAPTER TWO

The Changing Styles

'That is not my style at all,' a man may say, and in so saying he infers that to him style is a personal thing, representing what he likes or does not like. But style is not static, and in ceramics, as in everything else, it is continually changing as the old and familiar gives place to something new and refreshing. Sometimes, of course, change is compelled by some outside influence, as we have seen so recently in the return to simple, undecorated 'utility' wares, but more often it is the inevitable result of changing fashion in a wider sphere than that of pottery and porcelain. Sometimes, even, it denotes a change in the entire outlook of a nation. How else can one express the characteristic spirit of the Victorian era, which manifested itself in every aspect of human activity and art? There is another meaning of the word 'style' when it is applied to our particular subject, for it may express the knowledge and the tradition which have accumulated since the days when men first began to work in clay, the experience which has been gained of shape, texture, and decoration over the past centuries, and which has been passed on. In this sense, by style we mean a knowledge and appreciation of material, which will allow of nothing which is alien to its limitations. It is necessary for us to bear in mind both these definitions, even though for the purpose of our discussion we must adopt the chronological meaning, and reserve the other as a yardstick by which to measure excellence.

In the first sense it is clear that styles cannot be clearly bounded. There must inevitably be survivals, usually for sentimental reasons and, therefore, popularity, for why else has the 'willow pattern' survived for nearly 200 years? There must be revivals, such as the modern return to the practical, clean austerity of the old creamware designs, and the gayer colourfulness of modernized versions of the patterns of Worcester, Bow, and Chelsea. In ceramics as in any other form of art, periods or styles must unfailingly overlap, and there must always be the occasional unique peculiarities of a particular decorator or factory which may be alien to the style of the moment.

Since our attention is restricted to porcelain there is much of value in the history of English potting which must escape deserved and detailed study; much, too, which is most essentially native both in conception and in execution and which may have considerable bearing or influence on porcelain making. Nothing can excel the true, unpretentious wares of the mediaeval potter, with his nice appreciation of the forms and decorations most suited to his medium, and no ware more epitomizes the bluntness and straightforwardness of the British character than the lead-glazed Tobies and figures of the Woods. Even the tin-glazed delft, copied though it was from alien sources, commemorates an indomitable struggling towards an unattainable ideal. But our earthenware makers possessed that tradition of which we have already spoken, whereas the first English porcelain makers had a two-fold problem to study and, finally, to overcome. In the first place, they had to find out how to make a body which would emerge intact and reasonably shapely from the kiln, and that was no easy task. This done (and many fell by the wayside in the doing), they had to decorate it. Contemporary advertisements show that decorators were sought who had had previous experience in painting upon 'china', and it is certain that those who had painted on delft in the potteries of Liverpool, Lambeth, and Bristol would be most welcome. Those, at any rate, were accustomed to working upon a white surface, although their enforced bold, sweeping style was perhaps ill suited to the more fragile and delicate porcelain, which had to compete with and even to rival the Chinese and Continental wares which had already attained near perfection. One advantage they had, nevertheless, in the possession of a vocabulary of designs and patterns. They had inherited, at second or even third hand, a tradition of decoration which could be adapted to the new ware, and in any case, when porcelain was judged by the standard of foreign work it would have been bad policy to have attempted anything new in the way of ornament, for the public wanted that to which it was used, or something as near like it as possible. Thus, until porcelain was an accepted and commonplace household commodity, there was no native English style, and decoration was copied from whatever sort of ware was in fashion on the Continent, even though at the same time it was often anglicized in the copying.

The Chinese Influence

The earliest period of English porcelain saw the making of wares almost exclusively decorated in the Chinese style, for two reasons already mentioned. There was the first-hand influence which resulted from the presence in Europe of large quantities of comparatively inferior Chinese porcelain, mostly painted in blue, but also occasionally in colour, and in this country of Continental porcelain decorated in a similar style. Then, too, if the view is accepted that our porcelain was a logical development of the earlier imitative ware, delft, it is to be expected that its decorators would use the same designs. It is natural that our native workmen should have been always a step behind their fellows across the Channel, for the spread of ceramic knowledge was Westward, and the first English styles of the 1750s were those of Meissen, for instance, of thirty years before.

Before an attempt is made to understand the English versions of the Oriental, it is important to have a clear understanding of the spirit of all Chinese art, a spirit which is inseparable from legend and fairy story, from tales of painted dragons on silk and porcelain attracting rain in times of drought, and from creations which came to life for the pleasures of an imperial patron. But apart from this fanciful aspect of their art, the Chinese artists worked to a set of rules known as the Six Canons, from which they seldom departed, and a knowledge of which helps the European to understand their creations. They are as follows:

1: vitality and rhythm
2: accurate anatomical structure
3: a likeness to nature
4: suitable colouring
5: balanced composition
6: imitation of the antique.

In some respects the first is by far the most important, and may be compared with the modern emphasis on the drawing of what is felt rather than what is seen. A Chinese painting is above all the expression of a mood, of a spirit rather than of a substance. In this regard, how far short of the original landscape which inspired it falls the typical 'willow pattern' design! Take, for example, a painting of this type which may be seen on many a piece of K'hang H'si 'blue-and-white'. We look at the panorama of winding river with its infinite detail of forest, bridges, lakes, and tiny houses – here the water foams angrily, or swirls over hidden rocks, or here it flows placidly past a little village. But always, finally, it leads to the silent, remote mountain peaks, or loses itself in the mists of the distant sea. The mood is that of tranquillity. Every painting is at once a poem and a journey through life, and in each we find the Canons faithfully observed, the vibrant lines of wheeling birds (each a masterpiece of keen observation), the foliage of a tree, the perfect balance of a composition exactly suited to the shape containing it, and all drawn with rare economy of line and colour.

The Chinese artist at his best has a spontaniety and vigour of line which is closely related to Chinese calligraphy, from which these same two attributes are inseparable. The poet Tu Fu once said 'It takes ten days to paint a rock', and we can well under-stand his meaning, for without long observation and an exact eye-picture of that rock it would never be possible to represent it by means of the few swift, sure brush-strokes which bring it to life so vividly. There is never any hesitancy, and never an erasure. On the other hand, just as an apparently spontaneous picture was the result of a long self-discipline to established rule, so were the exquisitely placed brush-strokes themselves, for they had their names – the 'axe-cut', the 'mouse-tail', and so on, the swift, slashing impulsiveness or, at the other extreme, the tenuous, slender delicacy of a hair.

Such was the spirit behind the art of the Oriental decorator, whether he worked on silk, lacquer, or porcelain, and it is easy to appreciate why a copy, however careful, could never quite retain it. That is why neither the export wares made for the European market, nor the Japanese copies, are representative of the best.

What sorts of subjects were used as the inspiration of the Chinese porcelain painters? The answer must, perhaps, be prefaced by the observation that the finest wares are those which were seen even less 200 years ago than they are nowadays, because they were not intended for everyday use, but as ceremonial vessels, gifts for influential persons, or treasures to be appreciated only by the connoisseur. Nevertheless, the styles of decoration applied to them were representative of those which were more widely used on commoner wares, and which may now be briefly described.

The Chinese painter intended his motifs to have definite meanings, to point out morals, or to serve as reminders of some religious or ethical truth. Thus we find that, by and large, most of the 18th-century designs which were available to European artists had their early origins in religion, ceremonial, or myth, even though their deeper symbolism was often no longer understood, and their forms inaccurately preserved. A further point which must not be overlooked is that the western market had considerable influence on the sort of patterns which were placed upon the wares intended for it, as may be seen from a translation by S. W. Bushell of the *Discussion of Pottery* by T'ao Shuo. In 1774 this Chinese authority wrote that 'out of ten designs you will get four of foreign colouring, three taken from nature, two copies of the antiques, and one from embroidery or brocade.'

The earliest religious motifs are naturally found more often on pottery and stoneware, but among those favoured by the porcelain painter we find the following. The Eight Trigrams, each consisting of three unbroken or differently divided lines, intended to represent the Elements. The Chinese Dragon, perhaps the most copied of all, with serpentine, scaly body and scowling face, personifying the powers of the air, the rain, and the storms, and for ever in pursuit of the sun, in the shape of a flaming pearl. The five-clawed version was the symbol of the Emperor himself, though it is improbable that pieces bearing it were reserved for his sole use. The Empress, too, had her own symbol in the form of a Phoenix, and it is interesting to surmise that the many European versions of the pheasant or the peacock, or even the 'exotic bird', may have had their beginnings in this fabulous creature. At the entrance to many a temple the Dogs of Fo were to be seen, the guardians of the sacred place and, on porcelain, of a precious piece, not to be confused with the Kylin, who was the emblem of True Perfection. It is a far cry from such as these to the Staffordshire dogs which still guard the hearth of a cottage, and which are their direct descendants. The Yin Yang, a circle divided into two equal comma-shaped spaces, is the sign of the duality of existence – male and female, fire and water, night and day, and this, too, is a common enough decoration in modern days.

Buddhism invaded China during the first century of the Christian era, and some of the finest early figures were made in the likeness of the various deities associated with it. So far as painted decoration is concerned it is more usual to find representations of animals or objects which were in some way identifiable with the Buddha's life, as for instance the Hare which, according to legend, offered itself to him for food. The Eight Buddhistic Emblems are comparatively common, above all the Lotus, a flower which arises in splendour from the river mud, and so became the symbol of Purity. It is often replaced by the somewhat similar stylized chrysanthemum. The Wheel, the Conch Shell, the Umbrella of State, the Canopy, the Vase, the Pair of Fishes, and the Endless Knot (or Entrails) complete the list. Yet another collection of objects, the Seven Gems, was intended to represent the equipment of the all-powerful ruler, the magic-working Jewels, the General, the Horse, Elephant, Girl as perfect as Jade, Golden Wheel, the Keeper of the Treasure.

The cult of Longevity was introduced by the Taoists, and by the 18th century many symbols associated with it were in common use, such as the Tortoise, the Hare, the Chrysanthemum, the Gourd, the Prunus, the Pine, and, of course, the Eight Im-mortals themselves, usually pictured in some scene or incident connected with their fabled lives. The followers of Confucius, on the other hand, revered all Learning, and there is a host of legends about poets and scholars who were immortalized in every branch of art. On porcelain, as a rule, the chosen hero was depicted as the central figure in copies of classical landscapes, complete with fishermen, pagodas, willows, wheeling birds, and boats. The Chinese reverence for scholarship and for precious things of the past is exemplified in the well-known and often copied 'Hundred Antiques' decoration – the hundred signifying 'many', and not the exact number. From this larger collection the 'Eight Precious Things' were selected for the highest praise, the Jewel, the Coin, the Lozenge of Victory, Jade, the Artemesia Leaf, the Horns of Fertility, the Pair of Books, and the Painting, all of which are to be found not only in the decoration itself, but also in the most honourable place of all, beneath, in the form of the Mark. We find many other symbols of learning and of rank (since the two were considered synonymous), such as the mandarin's sign of the Vase and Feathers, the Ink and Brush of the poet or the artist, the Coral of long life (and increasing wisdom), and the Eight Musical Instruments. Accomplishment in the arts was symbolized by a Lyre Case, a Checkers Board and Box for the pieces, a Pair of Books, and a Pair of Scrolls, because a Chinese painting took the form of a journey upon which the eye travelled as the scroll was unrolled. Everything in a landscape may have significance, for even the sun, moon, stars, the mountains, or the grass were included among the Twelve Ancient Ornaments of the all-powerful and godlike Emperor.

Animals and birds were commonly featured on porcelain, for a very interesting reason apart from their decorative value. The Chinese language is monosyllabic, and a spoken character has many meanings, so that there is abundant opportunity for punning upon a word. The picture of a deer, translated into sound, will also signify Advancement, a fish will read as Fertility, and a bat may give the promise of Blessings.

The sure, exquisitely placed brushwork of the Chinese painter is nowhere seen to better advantage than in flower painting, and a great deal of Chinese ware bears studies of plant life, in which symbolism is abundantly present. Apart from the fact that every month of the year has its own particular flower, a complete picture may tell a story, as we see in the 'blue-and-white' 'Cracked Ice' pattern which was copied at Worcester, in which the coming of spring is commemorated by the white hawthorn blossom upon the breaking ice of the river. When flowers are used by themselves there is usually an entire absence of equally spaced, geometrical arrangement. Instead, we see a studied lack of balance, an asymmetry in which a flower-spray may curve gracefully to follow the swelling of a bowl or the depression of a plate, enhancing the purity of the white space without attracting undue attention to itself. We see the painting as an intrinsic part of the whole, and not as something apart to be admired for its own sake. Such superior forms of decoration were adopted, wisely, by our own 18th-century painters.

The use of diaper patterns and borders in Chinese style has continued to the present day, patterns which had their origin in the ancient symbolism found on vessels of bronze, and which were later adapted for use on silks and brocades. In the various stages of development they became more or less conventionalized, and were given such names as 'fish-roe', 'trellis', or 'fish-scale'.

It has already been said that much Oriental porcelain found its way into Europe, by various overland or sea routes. Some of it, though not all, was made specially for export, as for example a garniture of vases which could be intended for nowhere but a European mantelpiece, handled tea-cups, and flat-rimmed plates. But apart from special shapes there were also special decorations, because the Western middlemen would supply specimens or drawings of whatever sort of pattern their customers had ordered. Whole services of armorial china were made for the English gentry – one can picture the dismay of the perhaps legendary householder whose motto 'I think, I thank', roughly pencilled beneath his sample sketch, was translated on every piece of his enormous and costly service into the astonishing 'I stink, I stank'. Much of the so-called 'Chinese Lowestoft' porcelain is of this armorial type, probably painted at the decorating establishments of Canton, to where it was sent in the glazed white state from the potteries of Ching-te-chen. We find patterns accompanied by inscriptions in French and in Dutch, copies of 18th-century French engravings, classical scenes, and a host of Christian subjects on ware which has been called 'Jesuit China', from the fact that two Jesuit priests worked as painters at the Imperial Court in the 18th century. Even blue-printed English porcelain was copied, with the result that it is possible to see a Chinese painted copy of a printed 'willow pattern' landscape.

There is space only to mention briefly the colours in which all these styles of decoration were executed. The 'blue-and-white' has already been discussed, and in addition there were enamels. Broadly speaking, pieces painted in them may be divided into three classes – 'famille verte', 'famille noire', and 'famille rose', so called because of the colour usually predominant in each class. The first of the three originated in the 'san ts'ai', or three colour wares of the Ming period, to whose green, yellow, and purple were added an overglaze red and underglaze blue, thus forming a five colour palette. Occasionally an emphasis on the yellow enamel gave rise to a new name – 'famille jaune', while on the other hand a specimen may possess all the characteristics of its 'family' and yet have no green colouring at all. The 'famille noire' is also really a branch of the same family, but pieces belonging to it bear a particularly lustrous black which is not actually an enamel in the true sense of the word, but an underglaze dull black over which has been washed a thin green glaze. Practically the whole range of subjects was carried out in the 'famille verte' style, and the effect of the wonderfully fresh-looking, brilliant enamels is indescribably gay and colourful, especially when they were applied in white panels reserved against a powder-blue ground. A typical example of 'famille verte' colouring is to be seen on the famous 'Bishop Sumner' service made at Worcester,[1] but in comparison the enamels are lamentably dull and uninteresting. Towards the end of the K'hang H'si period the 'famille rose' began to replace the 'famille verte' in popularity, its distinctive feature being a pink enamel derived from gold. Pieces of this class were much copied at Bow [13],[2] above all other

[1]Frank Lloyd Collection, no 2; *Worcester Porcelain*, Hobson, pl xxxv.
[2]Figures within brackets refer to plates at the back of this book.

factories, with the same white and aubergine, but here again the colours are muddy in comparison with those, for example, which are seen to perfection on the egg-shell 'ruby back' plates of the Chinese.

Brief mention must be made of certain Japanese porcelains which were copied in this country, the so-called Kakiemon wares [11–12.] Kakiemon was a 17th-century Japanese potter who originated a series of rather slight designs in bluish-green, soft Indian red, pale blue, pale yellow, and gold. There was usually a central motif in the shape of a spray of flowers, a fantastic bird or animal, or an Oriental figure, with a narrow floral or diaper border in red and gold. This Arita ware (or 'Old Imari', as it is sometimes called) developed later in the 18th century into a coarser, greyish ware, decorated with a hotch-potch of brocaded pattern in muddy blue, red, and gold, which often covered the entire surface of the porcelain. The Chrysanthemum was a common subject of decoration, either in natural or stylized form. It is said that a Dutchman, Sieur Wagnar, persuaded the Japanese so to pander to Western taste, but the results of his enterprise are not accepted as true art by the educated Oriental.

The English artists on the whole showed fine discrimination in their choice of models from the Kakiemon designs – the 'wheatsheaf' [12] and 'partridge' [or 'quail'] patterns [11] are well known on the Worcester and Bow porcelains. We read, indeed, in the Bow advertisements of 1758 of the making of 'a large assortment of the fine enamel and fine Partridge sets'. At the same time, we should distinguish between such as these and certain others which are given the vague name of 'Japan' [17–24], which may embrace Chinese and Japanese designs as well as others of European invention. The revival of Japan patterns early in the 19th century resulted in a host of gay but entirely meaningless examples, especially at Derby, where in 1847 Bloor advertised for 'twenty good enamel painters who can paint different Japan patterns.'

The Meissen Influence

This section, which deals with the Meissen influence from 1760 to 1770, will necessarily be a short one, because so many of the Meissen styles were themselves copies of the Oriental ones. The famous factory was founded as early as 1710, and it was to be expected that its porcelain would dictate the fashion in the new ware. That this state of affairs did not continue was entirely due to the taking over of the pottery by the Prussians in 1763, with a resultant delay in reorganization which allowed the Sèvres concern to replace it in the forefront of ceramic fashion. Even so, before that disaster, French customs, taste, and even language had had considerable influence on every aspect of German culture, including painting on porcelain.

It was a characteristic of all the German factories that production was economically planned with typical Teutonic thoroughness, and little initiative was left to the individual. Thus, at Meissen, there was an art director, who from his library of pattern books, engravings, paintings, and specimen pieces dictated the chosen styles of decoration. In the early days, in what is known as the Baroque Period, the emphasis was on heavy, rather overpowering decoration, to give way later to the naturalistic flower painting and fanciful scrolls of the Rococo. In turn came a revival of French taste known as the Louis Seize Period, with its garlands of flowers and silhouette portraits, its sentimentality, and its general lightness of touch and tasteful colour. From one or other of these periods came those styles most commonly copied in this country, of which the following is a brief list:

1) formal Oriental flowers, the 'indianische Blumen', which later became the 'Indian Flowers' of the Potteries;
2) naturalistic flowers, or 'streu Blumen', with winged or other insects, the chief source of inspiration at most of the early factories;
3) idealized flowers, or 'Meissner Blumen', in bouquets;
4) naturalistic birds, as stiff and formal as those in a text book;
5) 'exotic birds', or 'fantasievögel', entirely imaginative, but gay, and full of movement;
6) pseudo-Chinese landscapes and figure subjects in brilliant enamels;
7) European landscapes and harbour scenes, in monochrome or polychrome;
8) copies of Kakiemon patterns.

It is clear from this list that it must often be quite impossible to say whether painting on an English piece has its origin at first or second hand, even though we may occasionally read such an advertisement as that of Derby, in 1758, when the 'second Dresden', or porcelain 'as finely painted as Dresden' was praised. It is true to say that the Meissen art directors, especially Johann Gregor Herold, who began work in 1720, succeeded in founding a school of European decoration which might well have served as the inspiration for practically everything copied by the Englishmen, though there are still many English patterns copied from the Oriental which are not to be found on Meissen wares.

Most of the Meissen decoration was carried out in enamels, for even underglaze blue could with difficulty withstand the high kiln temperature necessary for the fusing of the very refractory paste and glaze. This circumstance led to the selling of a great deal of glazed white ware to outside decorators known as 'Hausmaler', whose work is, of course, too varied and individual to be discussed here. For the same reason ground colours were not used extensively, though a good carmine pink was known before 1720, and turquoise, dark blue, yellow, and green within the succeeding twenty years. Scale-blue, copied from the Chinese, is sometimes found on Meissen porcelain.

The Sèvres Influence

The Sèvres styles are to be seen on the English porcelain of the last thirty years of the 18th century, and they constitute the last foreign influence over its ornamentation. The industry in France, and especially at Sèvres, was the pampered protegée of the aristocracy. No excuse was spared to make a paste which has never been excelled, and the finest artists were engaged to paint upon it. According to Binns, the successful imitation of old Sèvres was the ultimate goal of every Worcester painter. Sèvres porcelain, moreover, apart from its excellence, is outstandingly symbolic of French society at that time, with its gaiety, its daintiness, its colourfulness, and its brittleness.

If there were one attribute of Sèvres which others strove to rival, it would be the extensive range of lovely ground colours which were easily applied to the 'soft' body and which showed to such softly glowing advantage upon it. The most outstanding of these were as follows:

bleu-du-roi, introduced about 1750 to replace the old gros-bleu of Vincennes;
bleu celeste, or turquoise, first used in 1752, and shortly followed by jaune jonquille, a lovely yellow;
apple-green, about 1756, in the imitation of which the English chemists found their pea-green, sea-green, and many others;
Rose Pompadour, in 1757, often wrongly called Rose Dubarry, for the Dubarry did not appear at Court until 1770; this fine colour was the invention either of Xrowet or Hallot, it is not certain which.

At a later time these were supplemented by other colours which had been adapted to the 'hard' paste of the 1770s and onwards, such as the fond écaillé (tortoiseshell), dark blue, aubergine, pink, brown, yellow, and black.

Ground colours were used either plain or decorated with gold diaper, of which there are many varieties. 'Oeil de perdrix' was formed of rings of gold dots enclosing white circles [59], and it was used commonly on blue or turquoise; ovals of various sizes formed into a network made the tracery known as caillouté (pebbled) [89]; rivers of gold surrounding islands, like mud-flats at low tide, vermiculé [135]. Added to these were countless arrangements of trellis, spiders' web, dots, and stars. In the majority of cases the colours were used to frame white reserves decorated with a large range of subjects, chief of which, from our point of view, is flower painting, whence the Chelsea painters, in particular, derived their styles and palette, which they later took to Derby and Worcester. Festoons of flowers and trellis inspired the 'hop-pole' of Worcester in its several varieties, their 'exotic birds' were copied from Meissen, and their rustic figures (or fancy-dress versions of them), classical scenes, and figures were painted after Boucher or Watteau, and are redolent of the carefree, artificial spirit of Fragonard.

With the gradual disappearance of the 'soft' paste body many changes took place. The modification of the ground colours was not always successful – turquoise and *Rose Pompadour* in particular became dull and lifeless shadows of the originals, and were finally abandoned – the colours showed less brilliantly and yet at the same time more garishly. Above all, the easier manipulation of the new paste enabled the potter to indulge the craze for importance which was coincidental with the classical revival which swept across the Continent. Enormous vases, often mounted in ormolu, became the chief product of the factory, as befitting the pomposity of the Napoleonic era, and a search for anything really worthwhile yields little result, if we except the introduction about 1780 of the 'jewelled Sèvres' which was imitated successfully by the Worcester potters from about 1820 onwards [119]. In keeping with the inevitable time-lag, it was not until the latter half of the 19th century that English potters gave full attention to the large vases and the ormolu, notably at Coalport, though, of course, on the whole the early part of the century brought with it the results of mastery of potting technique and the resultant emphasis on excessive decoration.

On the 'hard' paste classical vases of Sèvres careful but often laboured decoration was painted, often covering the whole surface as Empire taste demanded, and so it was on the English imitations. The ground colours were copied and new ones were discovered, together with landscapes, figure subjects, flowers, and 'exotic birds'. Dress services were made for the country squire as well as for the nobility, often with elaborate coats-of-arms, and usually with the gadrooned edges copied from silver, the wide, coloured borders, and the heavy gilding. This was the age of the 'Derby Japan' patterns, and equally stiff and formal became the bouquets of flowers and the birds, however much they may still be admired for their technical perfection. Only in the realms of domestic wares for ordinary people may simplicity be found, in the fluted, sprigged designs, or in the artless copies of late 18th-century imported Chinese tea wares, with their sketchy ribbon or dotted line borders, and little sprays of blobbed flowers.

The Later Years

It is difficult to do more than to indicate the general trend of decoration on the porcelain of the 19th century, which saw the final stage of the change from the individualism of the early days to the mutual co-operation of modern times. Some of the early factories still survived, notably at Derby and at Worcester, but those were exceptions lying outside the great industrial region of the Potteries, and preserving, as a result, their own individual traditional styles while jealously guarding their new ones. Broadly speaking, it was still an age of emulation of the past, but it was also one of attainment to that degree of technical mastery which paradoxically deprives the later wares of much of the fascination possessed by the old. This mastery was abundantly apparent at the Great Exhibition of 1851 which showed, above all, how extravagant and fantastic decoration could be. It was a display which catered for those able to buy expensive porcelain, and for those who wished its value to be apparent. Mechanical processes removed more and more those defects which were the results of limited knowledge, the variations in colour tone, the inequalities of surface, and the warping. Nevertheless, than as now, the artist had to use materials which did not allow of error or erasure, and this fact should not be forgotten in our judgement of his skill.

Interspersed here and there in the long period of emulation, imitation, and revival it is to be expected that there would be isolated introductions of something new. Thus we find the 1842 'Parian' body of Minton, the imitation mother-of-pearl of the Irish Belleek, and the later 'ivory' body of Worcester, all calling for suitable decoration upon them.

To sum up, it is clear by and large that the style of decoration on English porcelain, in the earlier days at any rate, was dictated by that of the foreign wares which were imported in their turn into this country. Contemporary judges and purchasers were as ever eager to applaud the latest fashion, although looking back we may sometimes think that their admiration was misguided. We should not forget, too, that an occasional pattern or style was evolved from our native pottery; indeed, the idiom of its decorators has never been entirely lost, but crops up unexpectedly on porcelain right up to the present day. It is worth remembering, perhaps, that in ceramics as in everything else in life, that which is novel is invariably popular even before its real worth has been proved.

CHAPTER THREE

'Blue-and-White' Porcelain

Any account of the early wares decorated in underglaze blue must necessarily stand somewhat apart from the general plan of these pages, and must at the same time be shorter than its extensive subject deserves. In the first regard it is obvious that the very nature of 'blue-and-white' makes a separate chapter essential; it is different in so many ways, in its appearance, its technique, its fundamental simplicity and austerity of design, and its comparatively limited, clear-cut boundaries of period. It originated, as we have seen, for reasons of popularity, and it continued in favour for a long time because it was cheap to produce, especially in printed form. When at last it was discontinued, it was because familiarity brought with it sophistication and a desire for colour.

Some years ago I wrote an account of English 'blue-and-white' in which I expressed the opinion that it had been undeservedly neglected and that its virtues were unappreciated, and I have no reason to change my mind. The Chinese realized that no other colour provided a more perfect foil to the pure white body of their porcelain, and their artistry ensured that underglaze blue decoration never detracted from it, or from the invariably tasteful shapes into which it was potted. They, of course, had the secret of the blue, which our own chemists seldom discovered. Nevertheless, despite the large variety of hues which are to be seen on our native wares, the greys, the indigo, and the violet, the tradition of restrained design was continued, at least as far as Chinese motifs are concerned, and in that restraint lies the attraction and the aesthetic worth of our 'blue-and-white' from about 1750 to the end of the century.

Many of the styles of painted decoration were imitated in transfer printing, although the former are superior in every regard save that of original cost. The engraver, working on a flat surface, was unable to design for any particular shape of vessel; that part of the work was left to the decorator, who cut and pieced his transfers to the best advantage. Furthermore, the charms of graded colour-washes and flowing line were entirely lacking in the mechanical line-shading and cross-hatching of an engraving, however well cut, a fact realized perhaps by the Lowestoft blue-painters who sometimes added colour-washes to their printed designs.

Before listing the most well known of the 'blue-and-white' designs it is necessary to make some mention of the relationship between printing and painting. As we have said, the introduction of overglaze printing in enamels did not long precede printing in underglaze blue, which was probably in full swing by the end of 1760. It was too good an opportunity to miss, and we know that Richard Holdship, leaving Worcester in 1759, knew the process sufficiently well to be able to try it out at Derby in 1764, though with little success through no fault of his. At Worcester then, and at Caughley, cheaper versions of the popular blue-painted wares were produced; the latter factory was, in fact, given over almost entirely to printing, both on its own porcelain and on that of Worcester. Of Liverpool, or at least of its numerous and scarcely identifiable factories, we know very little, save that a great deal of printed ware was made, as might be expected from the city where Sadler and Green were in business. Lowestoft blue-printing was not successful enough to warrant its general adoption, the prints usually seen are almost entirely floral in conception, and show a hesitancy in execution which betrays a lack of skilled engravers.

Underglaze Blue Painting in the Chinese Style

LANDSCAPES Actual copies of original Chinese landscapes or water scenes are very rarely found on English wares. Indeed, it would almost seem that the Western artist had his own ideas of what Chinese decoration ought to look like, and his own opinion of the features looked for by his customers. The result was a series of pictures which contained all the ingredients of the originals, the characteristic pagodas, trees, flowering shrubs, fences, and bridges which, though generally Oriental in appearance, were yet lacking in the spirit of the symbolical Chinese wares [4].[1] Some of the designs were carefully drawn, such as those created by the Worcester artist whose 'mark' was the Chinese symbol for 'jade'. Others were conceived on a broader, bolder scale, with economical sweeping brush-strokes after the manner of a delft painter [3], and others were elementary, almost crude, and clearly produced on wholesale lines with little pretension to artistic merit. Attempts have been made to classify the work of individual artists, and at Worcester and Bow, where work was signed with symbols and numerals respectively, this is sometimes possible. Otherwise, a distinctive method of painting trees, for example, may betray a painter's style – the 'stove-pipe' tree of Bow is a typical example. Again, the figures in a landscape may be as informative as the tent-shaped little gnomes of a Liverpool man. When all is said and done, painting in blue was not conducive to the development of individual styles, because cheap produc-

[1]Figures within brackets refer to plates at the back of this book.

tion meant piece-workers, and only on important pieces is truly outstanding work to be seen, however satisfying the ordinary domestic wares may be.

FLOWERS Here again it was seldom that exact copies were attempted, although the Chinese inspiration is often plainly apparent. This is particularly so when flower-sprays are used in conjunction with landscapes, with a graceful branch rising from a thicket to curl around the rim of a saucer or the side of a bowl, quite out of proportion but eminently satisfying. In the same way a single curling spray, crescent-shaped, was sometimes used, often with a peony as the central motif, in the simple style which characterizes some of the best Chinese of as long as 600 years ago. The peony, usually more or less stylized, was a favourite at Bow, just as at Worcester the lotus was preferred. We can see it in a very beautiful and well-known pattern used for dessert sets, in which concentric rings of petals ripple from a central single bloom, the whole painted in carefully graded washes of blue [5], for occasional attempts were made to imitate actual K'hang H'si pieces, not only as regards decoration, but paste also, and the exact slight blueing of the glaze. Flowers were used together with diaper pattern for rim borders, as in the *'ch'ing t'i pai hua'* of Worcester and Bow (in which the lotus is reserved in a *'joee'* sceptre-head), or as borders separating panels of 'Long Elizas'.

Inseparable from flower painting is a form of decoration called 'root ornament', featuring a peculiar rounded, irregularly shaped mass, usually pierced with several round holes, from which spring branches of flowering shrubs. Repeated copying without understanding sometimes resulted in the root becoming an erection shaped like a notice-board upon a post. This sort of design is effective because it is a focal point for well-balanced branches springing from it, and in common with the Chinese 'dragon' pattern it often possesses the peculiarity of continuing without interruption on the reverse side of a piece in typical Chinese manner.

CHINESE DRAGON The dragon Lung, of the Sky, chasing a pearl through the clouds, inspired this well-known pattern, which was common to Bow, Worcester,[1] Lowestoft, and Caughley. It should not be confused with the printed 'Broseley Dragon' of Caughley, which was probably derived from it, and which is a comparatively lifeless brute, woefully misshapen, and conventionalized out of all recognition.

'HUNDRED ANTIQUES' The Worcester version[2] is an exact copy of this Chinese design. Some of the instruments are quite recognizable, but others had lost their original shape before they reached Europe or, perhaps, were intended to be symbolical in the beginning. So scattered and disconnected is this pattern that it ought to be condemned, and yet, as so often happens, the result is pleasing. Time and time again the English artist or designer can point out so many impossibilities and yet, when he

[1]Fisher, pl 25*d*; Barrett, pls 50 and 51. [2]Fisher, pl 21.

attempts to re-draw a design according to modern rules the result is lifeless and unsatisfying.

'CRACKED ICE' This Worcester design [1] is truly representative of the Chinese use of symbolism, with its marbled blue ground and contrasting white prunus blossom, and the Chinese lady venturing forth to enjoy the spring freshness of her garden. The river ice is breaking, and the early-flowering plum blossoms are falling upon it from the trees above.

'LONG ELIZAS' The Dutch copied graceful Chinese ladies on their delft, and called them *lange liszen* (slender maidens), of which the English name is an obvious corruption. With the possible exception of Chelsea, where hardly any 'blue-and-white' was made, every porcelain bears them, either as part of a domestic scene or landscape, or as motifs in themselves, usually alternated with floral subjects in radiating panels. At Worcester one of the most satisfying designs was a garden scene, [2] featuring a woman and child, the latter holding a bird perched on a stick. From the same factory we have garnitures of vases and beakers painted with particularly tall and slender ladies in panels separated by foliate scrolls. [3]

'ELOPING BRIDE' OR 'LOVE CHASE' This is probably the most prized of all 'blue-and-white' patterns, and it is an exact Worcester copy of a K'hang H'si original of which there are several variations. The Chinese warriors and jugglers did not possess the romantic interest which has been given to them by European collectors, but the composition is well balanced and the subject interesting. [4]

'ST GEORGE AND THE DRAGON' A mug bearing this pattern and dated 1776 is in the Dyson Perrins Collection. It is interesting to wonder whether its true significance, the triumph of Good over Evil, was recognized by whoever gave it its equally appropriate English name. [5]

'THE JUMPING BOY' This pattern was used at Bow but also, occasionally, at Liverpool, possibly at Pennington's factory. The Chinese version clearly shows a little boy seated upon a bank, [6] but his attitude has changed through repeated copying without proper understanding of the subject.

'IMAGE' John Bowcocke, the travelling manager of the Bow factory, wrote in his memorandum book that 'they must all be the bordered image, blue and pale as you please', and it is clear that this design was a popular one. It is perhaps hardly necessary to point out that 'image' is a synonym of 'figure', referring to the warrior who is accompanied by his attendant, carrying his axe. [7]

'LADY WITH A KOTO' Many patterns personify the Chinese reverence for art and

[1] *Fisher*, pl 28. [2] *Idem*, pl 25b. [3] *Idem*, pl 1. [4] *Worcester Porcelain*, Barrett, pl. 43b.
[5] *Worcester Porcelain*, Hobson, pl XIX, no 6. [6] *Bow Porcelain*, Hurlbutt, pl 8b. [7] *Ibid*, pl 8a.

learning. In this particular instance, not only is the lady playing upon her instrument, for she is surrounded by a border of objects chosen from the 'Eight Precious Things'. This is a Bow pattern, and its exceptionally careful drawing is usually seen only on pieces made of the thinnest and whitest paste.

POWDER-BLUE The Chinese made frequent use of a powder-blue ground against which were reserved white panels containing decoration either in blue or in '*famille verte*' enamels. So far as the blue painting is concerned, there is little difference between the style of Worcester, Bow, Lowestoft, and Caughley; common to all is a round central panel in which is drawn a simple Chinese river scene with pagoda, tree, and fishing boat, surrounded by four fan-shaped reserves with river scenes alternating with tiny round ones containing flowers. This is the usual style, but there are two others peculiar to Lowestoft and Caughley respectively which call for special mention. At the former factory the reserves were sometimes misshapen, and are best described by saying that their borders, if they had any, would be composed of foliate scrolls.[1] At Caughley a completely new pattern was evolved which, though in Chinese taste, was probably a factory creation. In the centre is a large panel, circular or oval, containing 'root-ornament', flower-sprays, and a moth, and the rest is made up of alternate panels of powder-blue and white, the latter enclosing various patterns of diaper, stylized flowers, and Chinese emblems.[2]

Underglaze Blue Printing in Chinese Style

We have already said that the introduction of underglaze blue printing made it possible for imitations of the 'Blue Nankin' to be produced in large quantities. The connoisseur naturally appreciates the painted copies of the true K'hang H'si, but for the less enlightened a rather different sort of decoration proved more acceptable, a decoration which was a part of a wave of enthusiasm for anything remotely resembling the Chinese which showed itself in many a different guise. Chippendale designed his 'Chinese Chippendale' furniture to be in keeping with the japanned and lacquered cabinets in the great houses, and landscape gardeners planned the Chinese gardens outside their walls, culminating in the amazing Pagoda at Kew, a design by Sir William Chambers, the author of *Chinese Architecture* (1757). The man-in-the-street, for his part, demanded that his domestic china should be decorated in the same style, and such engravers as Robert Hancock designed their pseudo-Chinese prints, and copied from the French engravers such as Pillement.

[1]Fisher, pl 11. [2]*Idem*, pl 39.

'WILLOW PATTERN' Credit for this crowded miscellany of Chinese motifs has customarily been given to Thomas Minton, who learnt his engraving at Caughley before moving to Spodes in 1789. [1] Its overcrowded composition is quite un-Oriental, but the legend invented for it earned a popularity which has never waned. So far as porcelain is concerned it was virtually a Caughley monopoly, but its introduction at Stoke led to its later universal adoption on earthenware.

'BROSELEY DRAGON' The original painted dragon lost its realism and ferocity when it was adapted to printing at Caughley. [2] Nevertheless, as a design intended adequately to fill a space, particularly a circular one, it has much artistic merit, though never attaining the popularity of the almost contemporary 'willow pattern'. In common with the painted version, the pattern was so manipulated as to extend to the reverse of smaller pieces such as saucers or bowls, but on plates, for example, the whole was printed on the face.

'FISHERMAN' This very common pattern is of Caughley origin, [3] although it was sometimes copied at Lowestoft. It has several interesting features – the flower-spray curling out of all proportion from the root or rock, the fence in the foreground (which is a feature of many Chinese landscapes), and the 'cell and fleur-de-lis' border which is often seen also on Liverpool porcelain.

'LA PÊCHE' This is a Hancock design in 'Chinese Chippendale' style. [4] We know nowadays that no Chinese lady ever dressed in such a manner, but her head-dress is in a style which might have been expected in far-off Cathay, and the scrolled archway in the background is reminiscent of the rococo of many a gilded mirror of the period.

'LA PROMENADE CHINOISE' The clothes again, the umbrella, and the fence in the background like the back of a 'Chinese Chippendale' chair. [5] Hancock designed this, and the preceding pattern, especially for printing in blue, for the necessary use of shading was part of a technique which was alien to the clear-cut delicacy of line of the overglaze print.

FENCE PATTERN Both Worcester and Caughley used this adaptation of the Fisherman motif, but here the fence is zig-zag, and here again are the love-birds we see in the 'willow pattern'. [6] At Worcester the flower-spray is replaced by palm trees, [7] but always there is the crescent-shaped composition copied perhaps unconsciously from the Chinese.

'CHINESE GARDEN' Several versions were used at Caughley, [8] each featuring a woman and child, a large garden vase with flowers and fruit, smaller ones with large flower-sprays, and sometimes a tall tripod table in a style more English than Oriental.

[1] *Spode and his Successors*, Hayden, pl facing p 48. [2] Barrett, pl 21. [3] *Idem*, pl 17. [4] *Idem*, pl 29. [5] *Idem*, pl 30. [6] Fisher, pl 34b. [7] *Idem*, pl 34d. [8] Barrett, pl 18.

'VASE' There are unusual features in this Caughley engraving. [1] The vase itself which forms the central motif, the flowers, and the root ornament are washed in with pale blue, an expedient already mentioned in connexion with Lowestoft flower painting. In addition, the two flying bats for Good Luck supply a little piece of symbolism which is almost unique in blue-printed decoration.

'PAGODA' Very few Chinese styles were printed on Liverpool porcelain, and this is the best known of them, a Chinaman standing by a triangular erection like the gable end of a greenhouse [2], with a pagoda on an island in the left background. [2] There is a hint of the ground colours and scrolled reserves of the more aristocratic polychrome Chelsea and Worcester.

Blue Painting in Later Styles

By the time the Chinese influence was being ousted by those of Meissen and Sèvres, blue painting was rapidly passing out of fashion, and therefore owes comparatively little to the Continental factories. Nevertheless, some of the capable Meissen flower painting was copied on important pieces at Worcester, notably on the large and stately hexagonal vases, the mask-lipped 'cabbage-leaf' jugs, and the pairs of cornucopias. On such as these we may see wandering branches of flowering tree, with an occasional moth, butterfly, or other winged insect, or a flight of sketchy but vital birds. Sometimes, too, there are scattered flower-sprigs surrounding a central bouquet, or the sparse, straight-sided panels and sprays of the 'Copenhagen' or 'Imortelle' pattern [3] which was used to excess at the Thuringian factories, and copied at Lowestoft as well as at Worcester. It was, of course, natural that the elegant and colourful daintiness of Sèvres should have had little in common with English 'blue-and-white', and practically the only kinship was a result of the direct contact which was made by Turner of Caughley, when he visited the French factories in 1780. He brought back with him several French artists and some new ideas, so that we find certain 'sprigged' patterns such as the 'Chantilly Sprig' with a central cornflower, [4] and blue-painted versions of the festoons and garlands which are found in colour on the wares of Worcester, Derby, and Bristol. At this time, too, an added elegance was often given to Caughley porcelain by gilding applied outside the factory, which if anything detracts from the more ambitious patterns but which enhances the simpler, fluted and sprigged tea wares. Some of the latest, and certainly the rarest of 18th-century 'blue-and-white' was also made at the Salopian works, consisting of architectural subjects in

[1]Fisher, pl 36d; Barrett, pl 22. [2]Fisher, pl 43b. [3]*Worcester Porcelain*, Hobson, pl XIX, no 1. [4]Fisher, pl 41.

a very pale blue.[1] Lastly, we should make brief reference to a class of Worcester blue painting which really belongs to the enamelled work, since its flowers are rendered in a peculiar, vivid pigment called 'dry blue'. It will not live with the underglaze blue wares, but it is notable for its meticulous brushwork.

Blue Printing in Later Styles

Meissen flower painting was imitated on Worcester and Caughley blue-printed porcelain, in particular the large bouquets of flowers with moths and small sprigs,[2] and a more purely English creation, yet in the same unmistakable style, featuring medlars and a strange fruit resembling either a pine-cone or a mulberry – the well-known 'pine-cone' pattern which is the most common of all blue-printed decorations.[3] Sometimes the combination of English and Continental motifs is carried further, for we may see the Meissen flowers allied to English fruit and vegetables, or to trophies of arms like those found in colour on the later Sèvres. Printed versions of the 'sprigged' patterns, the 'Cornflower' in particular, were so well engraved that it is often difficult to distinguish them from the painted originals.

The emphasis on printing which was such a feature of the Caughley factory meant that an English tradition was fully established before the close in 1799. Later productions include several imaginary English landscapes (though with something vaguely Oriental about them),[4] and several views of the famous bridge at Ironbridge, which was finished in 1779 and which was the first bridge of iron to be built in the country.[5] Sporting prints in the style of Sadler and Green are common on both Worcester and Caughley wares.[6] Many of the Caughley designs which cannot be traced to any of the foreign influences were engraved by Robert Hancock, and still more are in his style although not definitely attributable to him. Among those which are in the former class are the 'Milkmaids',[7] 'Parrot and Fruit',[8] several 'Children's Games',[9] and a scene of ruins with a fisherman in the foreground.[10]

Border Patterns

There are literally scores of different borders on 'blue-and-white', ranging from the very elementary arrangements of cell-diaper, loops, ovals, circles, and dots, to the more elaborate ones of the 1780s.[11] Broadly speaking, the Oriental influence per-

[1]Barrett, pls 58 and 59. [2]Fisher, pl 31. [3]*Idem*, pls 33a and b. [4]Barrett, pl 19. [5]*Idem*, pls 23–25. [6]*Idem*, pls 27 and 28. [7]Fisher, pl 32. [8]*Idem*, pl 38; Barrett, pls 31 and 32. [9]*Idem*, pls 35, 38 and 39. [10]*Idem*, pl 34. [11]Fisher, figs 1–3.

sisted throughout, though later it was a bastard influence, with something in it of the decoration of 'export' wares, with its conglomeration of all sorts of diaper, flowers, butterflies, and scrolls. Only very rarely do we find a border which is suited to the main decoration, as, for instance, in the 'Milkmaids' pattern, with its border of alternate diaper, leafy scrolls, and panels of domestic animals. At the other extreme there is an occasional lack of any border at all, as in the 'Dragon' or 'root ornament' patterns, or, alternatively, a simple blue line.

Lovers of ceramics, whether collectors or not, are invariably clearly divided in their regard for 'blue-and-white' decoration. Leaving on one side the real interest which is inherent in its origin, it is really a question of the attraction of colour as opposed to the strength and simplicity of good design. This is not the place to argue the respective values of the two attributes (which indeed are married in the finest decoration), but it is significant, and an indication of popular taste, that when once the early wave of popularity had ebbed it was not until modern times that any sort of interest revived in blue painting or printing. Many contemporary patterns are copies of the old ones – the 'Willow Pattern', it seems, will never die – and new ones are usually based upon them, but it is perhaps unfortunate that the cheapness of blue-printing, in particular, has allied it to earthenware rather than to the finer body on which it was first placed.

CHAPTER FOUR

Early Overglaze Printed Decoration

We have seen how dependent our early porcelain makers were upon foreign methods and ideas. It is therefore a remarkable fact that within the space of fifty years the position became so very different, and the foreigners were forced not only to appreciate the great strides which had been made in the Potteries but also to adopt some of its ways. There is no need to dwell upon the nature of the revolution which took place during the latter half of the 18th century; one of its results was that decorative 'china' was no longer the prerogative of the well-to-do, but the everyday possession of ordinary people. The leisurely methods of the past had to give way to speedier mechanical processes, among which was the use of overglaze transfer printing.

The history of this class of decoration was until recently very obscure, but it has now been greatly clarified by the researches of modern writers, in particular Mr Cyril Cook (*Life and Work of Robert Hancock*). Concerned as we are with the results of the invention, it will suffice to say that enamel printing was introduced at Battersea in 1753 by John Brooks, to be adopted at Bow and, later, at Worcester during the following three years. It is certain that Hancock was responsible for that migration, as he was for the outstanding wares which resulted from it. At the same time, however, it should be remembered that much Liverpool porcelain was printed by John Sadler, though his work was less successful. Hancock, above all, was a true artist, not only in the expert use of his tools, but also in his sense of fittingness and balance, in his choice of subjects which would marry with the porcelain body, and in the tasteful adaptation of foreign ones. In his original work, too, in whatever style, the same attributes are invariably revealed, and this fact, apart from the lack of reliable information on his contemporaries, is sufficient reason for describing his work as most truly representative.

It is probably true to say that ultimate perfection in overglaze printing was reached soon after Hancock began work at Worcester – the well-known 'King of Prussia' mugs, dated 1757,[1] are clear evidence of a mastered technique, even though their aesthetic merits may be a matter of taste. We have already mentioned the similarity

[1]*Life and Work of Robert Hancock*, Cook, item 56.

between the Chinese (and the Worcester) black-pencilling and the finer examples of the black transfer print, a similarity which is all the more evident in Hancock's work because his black was really a black, with no trace of green or brown. Other colours used were lilac, brown, puce, and red, the last colour in particular on several of the prints best known on Bow porcelain, such as the 'Tea Party', 'L'Amour', 'Children at Play', 'The Prussian Hero', and several others, some of which are signed.

The first attempts are bound up with three factories, Bow, Redcliff Backs (or 'Lund's Bristol'), and Worcester, and it is necessary to understand clearly the order of events. First, as regards dates. The Battersea enamelling establishment closed in 1756, Hancock left for Bow and stayed but a few months before leaving for Worcester, and the amalgamation between the Bristol and Worcester factories took place in 1751. It follows, therefore, that the first prints are to be found on the Bow and Worcester wares of 1756, assuming that the printing was done inside the factory. Printing on porcelain is not the same as printing on enamels, because of the added problem of the glaze, which at Derby appears to have been insuperable. This fact goes far to explain why some of the Bow printing was clear-cut and delicate, whereas later work at Worcester was slight and seemingly inexpert. Compare the well-known Bow 'Aeneas and Anchises'[1] with the earliest Worcester examples,[2] the tiny prints of swans, squirrels, ships, and figure groups on early sauce-boats, with their unevenness of pigment and slight linear quality. The only explanation is that some difficulty was encountered in adapting the process to the rendering of the true black which was demanded at Worcester. At Bow the perfected work was printed in brick-red, a true black is rarely seen, and Hancock did not stay long enough to master its production, but at Worcester there was ample time for experiment in the shape of the tiny prints, which nevertheless were well suited to the moulded reserves in which they were placed. This moulding is usually found on pieces once thought to have been made only at Bristol, but the closure in 1752 makes it impossible for any printing to have been done there.

The almost contemporary production of perfected work at Bow and tentative attempt at Worcester was followed by innumerable prints in black and in other colours, and Hancock was catholic in his sources of inspiration, although many of his designs, as far as we know, were of his own invention. He contributed to such productions as *The Ladies' Amusement* (about 1760), *The Artists' Vade Mecum* (1762 and 1776), *The Compleat Drawing Book* (1762 and 1775), *The Compleat Drawing Master* (1753), and *The Draughtsman's Assistant* (1786), in many different styles, and many of the published designs are to be seen on porcelain, in underglaze as well as overglaze

[1]*Life and Work of Robert Hancock*, Cook, item 1. [2]*Ibid*, item 40.

28

form. A full list of the sources from which he drew his inspiration is to be found in Mr Cook's valuable book, and they may be roughly classified as follows:

The French School Boitard, Gravelot, Watteau, Cochin fils, Boucher, Lancret Chardin, Vivares, Le Bas, and de Larmessin;
The Italian School Jacopo Amiconi;
The German School Antoine Pesne;
Pseudo-Oriental Style Jean Pillement;
The English School Gainsborough, Ramsey, Barlow, James Seymour, Kent, Worlidge, McArdell, Walker, Houston, Hayman, Sullivan, Woollett, and Bickham.

In addition to recognizable copies or versions of works by these artists, here is a selection of engravings for which no origin has yet been found, and which may be assumed to have been Hancock's own creations.

'PARROT AND FRUIT' Probably the best known, and found in underglaze and underglaze form.
'THE TEA PARTY' There are several different versions of this design, but all feature the same Chippendale tripod table and sofa or, in a less intimate grouping, chairs.
'PHEASANTS' This design is clear evidence that the use of semi-exotic birds was not confined to coloured wares.
'MILKMAID AND GALLANT' The Watteau style is evident in this print, as also in the somewhat similar 'Milkmaid at the Gate'.
'GARDEN STATUARY' The clarity of line engraving, and the inclusion of such objects as a garden roller, a spaniel, and garden statuary, indicate that credit must be given to Hancock for this design.
'THE BIRD COOP' A rural scene in Dutch style, remarkable for the exceptionally able treatment of trees.
'FREEMASONS' EMBLEMS' The treatment of the foreground, with its characteristic shading and cross-hatching, is typical of Hancock's later work.
LANDSCAPES Nothing could be more charmingly appropriate for the decoration of a 'flat' piece of porcelain than the several designs of this sort, in which a small circular landscape is enclosed within a rococo border of scrolls and foliage.
'RUINS' There are several versions, although the name of 'Panini Ruins' is sometimes applied to them all. [137]

We cannot leave Robert Hancock's work at Worcester without mention of a class of decoration which is associated with James Giles, who owned a decorating establishment in London from about 1756 to 1776. His work will be discussed fully in a later chapter, but in this present regard it is on record that he bought black-printed wares (and occasionally those printed in other colours) over which he painted enamel colours. [1] He borrowed the idea, probably, from the Battersea enamellers, and although the effect is rather burdened the colours were well chosen and subdued, and the gilding tastefully sparse. The 'Tea Party', 'Ruins' [137] [2], and 'Milkmaids' [1] were the prints most often selected for this sort of work, and the results are interesting examples of an early attempt to marry the arts of printing and painting, which is not to be confused with quite another, and rarer technique which aimed at a similar result. Some years ago, in 1934, the late Dr Newman Nield spoke to the English Ceramic Circle about a small class of porcelain which he attributed to Bow, in which outline was faintly printed in colours, to be filled in with enamels. The outline, he found, was done in black, pink, and red, and Dr Nield pointed out that the use of a pink rather than a black line for roses, for instance, resulted in a much greater daintiness. Not until twelve years later did Mr Frank Tilley report several more pieces of the same sort (*Antique Collector*, September–October 1946), pieces decorated not only with flowers but also with landscapes and butterflies. Mr Tilley proffered the opinion that the entire class could possibly be ascribed to Chaffers' Liverpool factory, though there could be no absolute certainty. Against this suggested provenance is the fact that Bow specimens certainly exist which bear the same sort of decoration. Wherever the printing was done – and we cannot rule out the outside decorator – the technical difficulties of applying several different pigments to a single copper plate entirely ruled out the process as a commercial proposition, and it would seem that it was never developed past the experimental stage.

John Sadler was Hancock's contemporary and rival at Liverpool, and it is recorded that he printed porcelain between 1757 and 1763, in addition to his prolific work on creamware. In the former regard it has been stressed that although fine porcelain, well decorated, was undoubtedly made at Liverpool, very little is known about its many factories, and its wares have never been held in high regard. Because of this, Sadler and his work have naturally suffered neglect. Mention has been made of the difficulty of obtaining a true black, and Sadler experienced the same problem, for his became a faint sepia, or else was tinged with green, and he was really successful only with red. On porcelain, at any rate, there is nothing like Hancock's range of subjects; tea-wares sometimes bear a reversed form of Watteau's 'La Cascade', [3] a copy of the 'Tea Party', [4] and various other designs in the same pastoral style, which had been originally in-

[1] *Worcester Porcelain*, Hobson, pl L; Frank Lloyd Collection, pl 78, no 365; Herbert Allen Collection, pl 47, no 216. [2] Figures within brackets refer to plates at the end of this book.
[3] *John Sadler*, Price, pl 12. [4] *Ibid*, pl 12.

tended for tiles. There are several more ambitious prints to be seen on commemorative pieces, notably a 'King of Prussia' after Houston,[1] a 'George III',[2] a 'Queen Charlotte',[3] and a 'William Pitt'. This is admittedly a sparse and comparatively unimportant record, though its extent may be somewhat extended by the inclusion of prints by other engravers of lesser importance, such as Thomas Billinge, an outside engraver who at one time worked for Chaffers.

Hancock's departure from Worcester saw the virtual end of line engraving as a decoration in itself, and it was replaced by stipple engraving or, as it is usually called, 'bat printing'. There was sufficient reason for the change. The line engraving, even at its best, was incapable of expressing the delicacy of the new fashion of the end of the century, when the stipple engravings of the Bartolozzi and Angelica Kauffmann schools were becoming popular. Accordingly the line engraving press was replaced by the more sensitive pressure of the hand on a glue bat, other factories found themselves able to equal and surpass the best work of the line engravers, and the Worcester monopoly was a thing of the past. Flights certainly made extensive use of the new process, but it was in the Potteries that most advantage was taken of it, by Adams of Cobridge, where William Davis was the printer, by Baddeley of Shelton, at Mintons, and particularly at Spode, where gold bat printing was done. Outside the Potteries, good bat printing was done at the new Herculaneum factory, and at Swansea. Later developments are outside the scope of these pages, and may best be summed up by saying that line engraving continued as an aid to polychrome decoration, bat printing enjoyed a short popularity which did not long outlast the fashion it was designed to suit, and colour printing progressively gained ground as new pigments and processes were introduced.

[1]John Sadler, pl 13. [2]*Idem*, pl 14. [3]*Idem*, pl 15.

CHAPTER FIVE

The Oriental Styles

The fascination of Oriental decoration is difficult to define, but that it has always stood high in popular favour is shown by the persistence of Eastern motifs right up to the present day. In the earliest years, as we have seen, the Chinese wares in particular afforded the most readily available sources of design, but even when those of the Continental factories suggested new styles, the old ones were never completely abandoned, but rather were developed into more ambitious and splendid ones. Oriental porcelain of the highest class is above all things colourful – who has not seen a museum cabinet of the finest *'famille verte'* for the first time without a feeling of incredulity at the gaiety and freshness of the enamels – and the European chemists and artists were provoked to imitate, and to vie with each other in publishing the early results of their skill. Then we should not ignore the fascination of the East as it was seen and described by travellers, the land of spices and rare silks, of strange customs and fabulous monsters, a fascination which was not entirely lost when it was translated into the brushwork on a piece of porcelain, however inaccurate or misleading the result might be. The first painters summarized the characteristics of the wares they copied, and made for themselves a vocabulary which was sufficient to satisfy their equally ignorant customers – Chinese furniture, flowers, trees, birds, boats, and pagodas, with an occasional borrowing of the mosaic of a silken brocade. Sometimes they were able to copy exactly from an actual piece of *'famille verte'*, *'famille rose'*, or Kakiemon, but this was exceptional, and understandably difficult for us to trace.

'Mandarin' Patterns

It is natural that the most elementary patterns are to be seen on 'blue-and-white', not because enamelled ones were not made from the beginning, but because with few exceptions the cheaper ware was made for sale to a large public, and the decoration was done by a large staff of inexpert painters. In addition, when the completion of an intact and passably shapely piece of porcelain was a matter of some uncertainty, the additional hazard of the extra firing was something to be avoided. The paste and glaze sufficiently perfected, some of the earliest enamelled patterns were in the so-called

'Mandarin' style which we now describe. Its basis was the 'Long Eliza' or her male counterpart, featured in landscape or in interior scenes. As we have seen, the Chinese artist illustrated the myths and religions of his country, extolled its heroes, or paid homage to its respected arts or activities, but of these the imitator was ignorant, and his work was consequently more decorative than accurate. In his translations he usually missed the point, though naturally there were exceptions when careful and individual work was done. Yet another factor in the translation of the Oriental idiom was the copying of patterns from German or French porcelain, or from delft; it is indeed probable that comparatively few pieces were copied directly, but at second or even third hand, since fine pieces were simply not available in this country. The result was that alien styles were often married, and we may find, for example, Chinese landscapes and Meissen flowers in the same scheme of decoration.

It has been said by many authorities that to Worcester belongs the distinction of having produced the most faithful copies of every sort of Chinese decoration, and certainly the early Mandarin pieces made there, and at the earlier Redcliff Backs, fully justify that opinion. Let us deal first with the latter rather mysterious factory, about which so much has been conjectured but about which so little is really known. We are not here concerned with factory history as such, but it is a matter of relevant interest to trace the hazy beginnings of this Bristol 'fritt paste' venture, because they are bound up with lovely decorating. The visit of Dr Pococke to Bristol in November 1750 is well known and recorded, and his reference in a letter to 'a manufacture lately established here by one of the principals of the manufacture at Limehouse which failed'. Further evidence was unearthed by Mr Kiddell in the files of the *Daily Advertiser*, in which a request was made in January 1748 for the creditors of the 'Pot Manufactory at Limehouse' to meet upon 'affairs of importance'. That the meeting resulted in the closure of the London factory and in the opening of a new one in Bristol, by one of the partners, seems sufficiently probable, and gives the latter a life of about three years before Dr Wall took it over, with all its secrets, and continued its work at Worcester. Many names have been given to the little factory from time to time, but since it is acknowledged that its wares were made at a Glass House in Redcliff Backs the name of this vague locality would seem to be as fitting as any other.

Some of the porcelain made there has been identified on the evidence of marked pieces and contemporary writings, but it is plainly impossible to distinguish between late Bristol and early Worcester. Keeping this fact in mind we can read what Mr Honey has to say in his *Old English Porcelain*. He writes of a painter who used a very thin brush with remarkable skill, and of the gracefulness of his work, and that is a fair summary, though it omits other equally important features. For instance, the enamels

33

possess extreme brilliance, and composition is usually outstandingly good. The moulded reserves of the typical sauce-boats were admirably suited to the tiny landscapes with their deftly drawn figures, the enamels invariably soft in colour, but fresh-looking and translucent. [1] The general effect is difficult to put into words, but there is a certain gem-like quality which is seen also in much Chinese *famille rose* enamelling and, to a certain extent, on English enamelled salt-glaze of the finest quality. Attempts have been made to link this sort of work with the legendary Michael Edkins on the evidence of certain pieces of Bristol white opaque glass which were once the property of his grandson, William, and which were vouched for by him. A pair of bottles was exhibited at the National Exhibition of Art held at Leeds in 1868, and a note in the catalogue, by the same William, gave the information that 'a peculiar kind of white opaque glass, enamelled in colours, was made by Messrs Little and Longman and their successors Messrs Vigor and Stevens, at Redclyffe Backs. The principal enameller was Michael Edkins.' This particular pair was illustrated in the English Porcelain Circle's *Transactions* of 1929 [plate v], and described by Mr Wallace Elliot, and an exactly similar bottle, but of porcelain, is illustrated in Mr Honey's *Old English Porcelain* [1st edition, plate 57b]. The decoration on all three is exactly the same. Still further evidence is to be found in Owen's *Ceramic Art of Bristol*, in which mention is made of certain Bristol delft plates signed with the initials M^EB, of which the B was presumed to stand for Betty, Michael's wife. At first thought it would appear that there is circumstantial evidence to support the belief that Edkins, already proficient as a painter of glass and delft, turned his hand also to the decoration of the porcelain made at his old work-place. On the other hand, in his *English Delftware* Professor F.H. Garner dismisses Edkins in one short sentence; he has found little evidence to support the claims made on his behalf, and he illustrates only one piece of delft [2] which might possibly have been painted by him, on which the decoration bears little likeness to that upon the bottles. Again, Mr E.M. Elville, writing in *Apollo* in September 1947, stated that Edkins arrived in Bristol from Birmingham shortly before 1762, a date late enough to rule out any possibility of his working at the Redcliff Backs of pre-Worcester days. It is invariably dangerous to identify a painter's work by similarity of pattern on different pieces, for patterns, especially these simple early ones, can so easily be imitated. Accordingly, while we recognize the beauty of the Redcliff Backs painting, it is yet too early to give credit for it to any known decorator.

The established Worcester factory lost no time in making enamelled wares. In the present regard the simplest and perhaps the most charming patterns include groups of ladies and children painted in '*famille rose*' palette, with tables, tall tripods, and vases,

[1]Herbert Allen Collection, pl 45. [2]*English Delftware*, Garner, pl 74b.

with touches of gold here and there, and perhaps around the rim. No elaborate borders were used [8,][1] the whole effect being one of restful but bright masses of colour against a creamy paste which, for this particular sort of decoration, was left unblued.[2] From these simple beginnings developed a more crowded style, showing obvious Meissen influence, with similar figures in interior or garden scenes, but painted in panels reserved on various diaper grounds, or surrounded with gold scroll-work which also frames small sketches of landscape or flowers in red, pink, or black.[3] In both these sorts of design the figures are economically outlined and washed in with colour, but between 1760 and 1765, which is roughly their period, a style evolved which is markedly more ambitious and more detailed in the drawing. The robes of the 'Long Elizas' and the mandarins are shaded in well-drawn folds, the features full of character, and the hair strongly painted in intense black [9]. This main subject, and the usual accompanying smaller reserves, are surrounded by diaper grounds or scale pattern, or simply by one of the fine ground colours which were being introduced at the time.[4] No Worcester porcelain is more splendid, and certainly no style more tasteful. Sometimes, in keeping with Chinese practice, underglaze blue formed part of the palette, being used both for borders and in the figures and the furniture; indeed, it is common to find a blue design, in whatever style, which would be complete in itself (and is often found so on other pieces) which has had enamels added to it, a fact which has been taken advantage of by later 'clobberers' and fakers. Apart from patterns completely painted with the brush, the advent of overglaze printing brought with it the quicker application of outline, and both pinkish-brown and black were used at Liverpool and Caughley, as well as at Worcester. On the whole, whereas the earlier mandarins were repetitive copies of quite everyday Chinese patterns, albeit pleasing, dainty, and colourful, many of the later ones such as the rare 'Weaver' pattern were obviously exact copies of selected specimens which were not repeated on a large scale.

We shall see as we describe other sorts of decoration, that the Worcester styles afford an accurate cross-section of popular taste at any particular time; few were neglected, and nearly all were developed to an extremely high standard. For this reason there is little to be said about the mandarin patterns of other factories. Using the word Liverpool quite loosely we find that examples from one or other of the numerous factories bear the closest resemblance to those of Worcester [7], though the Chinese figures are usually crudely painted, with a greater use of heavy, black painted

[1]Figures within brackets refer to plates at the end of this book.
[2]Frank Lloyd Collection, pl 3, no 13; Herbert Allen Collection, pl 46, no 213.
[3]Frank Lloyd Collection, pl 3, no 21. [4]*Ibid*, pl 4, nos 24–26; Herbert Allen Collection, pl 50, no 289.

outline. A distinctive bright, flat red is another distinguishing feature. Nevertheless there are exceptions to the general rule, for it is becoming increasingly clear that it is unfair and unwarranted to saddle Liverpool with all the outcasts and the misfits. When Liverpool decoration is good, it is usually very good indeed, and some outstanding painting of Chinese figures must be credited either to Christian or to Chaffers, whose work was particularly influenced by Worcester [6]. The finest mandarin painting I have ever seen was on a large jug found many years ago by the late G. Owen Wheeler, whose pioneer insistence upon the possibility of Liverpool excellence is well-known. It was fully described and illustrated in the *Apollo Annual* for 1948 (page 59), its large, beautifully painted Chinese men and women, in true Chinese style with no trace of English translation about them, almost entirely covering the body of the piece. The enamels are still as glowingly colourful in clear greens, roses, and reds as the day they were applied, and this outstanding brightness of pigment is the most striking feature of the finest Liverpool decoration, adding weight to Wedgwood's reputed praise of Chaffers' enamels. The style of the delft painter is usually apparent, which is only to be expected when we consider that Liverpool was one of the strongholds of polychrome delft. We should look also for a comparatively washy, pale-greenish yellow, the washing over of foliage with a strong, transparent copper green, and clusters of bright red dots on the Oriental shrubs.

Most Lowestoft patterns are rather feeble copies of Worcester ones, and those of the mandarin class may usually be identified by their clumsiness of drawing and by the absence of the typical Worcester daintiness.[1] Frequent use was made of horizontal, broad, red-brown dashes on which the figures stand, and equally characteristic are the enamels in bright pink, a very vivid emerald-green, a thick, opaque blue, and a light red which is almost brown, a palette which would seem bound to clash but which is surprisingly effective. Always, too, there is to be seen that toylike quality in potting and in decoration which places Lowestoft porcelain in a class by itself.

Outstanding painting at Bristol and Plymouth is exceptional in this regard, for drawing is usually perfunctory,[2] with figures often grotesque, with swollen heads and splayed feet. The same may be said about the 'hard paste' wares of New Hall. The Bow artists concentrated on their flower painting, as we shall see, and apart from a few very early pieces painted with detached figures fashionable Chelsea scorned popular demand, though Duesbury's more plebian and commercial outlook allowed an occasional lapse in the Chelsea-Derby days. Later still he wisely realized that landscapes and flowers could sometimes give place to carefully drawn Chinese figures

[1] English Ceramic Circle Exhibition Catalogue, 1948, pl 109, no 477.
[2] *Champion's Bristol Porcelain*, Mackenna, fig 12.

painted in the extensive and colourful Derby palette.[1] In the Potteries, at Spodes, interpretation of mandarin styles was comparatively late, and outside our scope, since it coincided with the introduction of 'Stone China' by Josiah the Second in 1805. We are not concerned with earthenware, but the excellence of the designs applied to this clear, white body, with their marvellously wide range and always exact copying gives rise to regret that such effort was not expended on porcelain.

'Pencilled' Designs

Our knowledge of authentic Chinese decoration on porcelain is greatly augmented by reference to the official 'List of Decorations used on Imperial Porcelain in the Reign of Yung Cheng', in which is mentioned (no 40) designs which were 'painted in ink'. Père d'Entrecolles had something to say, too, about early attempts with organic inks, which, of course, disappeared in the kiln, before it was realized that metallic pigments had to be used for this as for all forms of ceramic decoration. Perfected painting in black outline is seen for the first time on the 'egg-shell' plates and cups of the Yung Cheng period (1723–35), and it was probably inspired by European engravings, copied line for line. Pieces of the so-called 'Jesuit' porcelain are typical examples. Sometimes it was inevitable that English decorators in turn copied Chinese designs which were themselves copies, as we see in such a piece as the saucer illustrated in Hobson's *Worcester Porcelain*, plate LIV, no 4.

Contemporary with the Oriental work a somewhat similar sort of decoration was carried out by a Bohemian *'hausmaler'* named Ignaz Preissler, who painted on Chinese, Vienna, and Meissen porcelain, but with few exceptions his work, called *'schwarzlot'*, was more intricately detailed than the first English attempts which followed thirty years later. There are two Chelsea plates in the Schreiber Collection painted in a similar style, one with a finely detailed view of Chelsea Parish Church, in black out-line, with applied washes of green.[2] Worcester, as usual, was first in the field with recognizable copies of the Chinese style, of which examples may be examined in the same Collection.[3] Patterns range from rather sketchy landscapes to figure subjects and stylized flowers and butterflies, and it is obvious that polychrome designs were some-times translated, apart from the copying of black-pencilled ones.[4] Most well known of all the Worcester patterns is that of the Chinaman with his ox, with a pair of anglicized, steepled buildings in the background,[5] but there are many others, all of them aesthetically satisfying in the contrast of bold, intense line against a creamy paste.

[1]*Crown Derby Porcelain*, Gillespy, pl 7, fig 11; pl 8, fig 12. [2]Schreiber Collection, pl 30, no 204. [3]*Ibid*, pl 56, no 511. [4]*Worcester Porcelain*, Barrett, pls 34–35. [5]*Ibid*, pl 35a.

Occasionally, too, a black-printed design is accompanied by a painted border of black diaper or conventional flowers. It was once thought that black pencilling in the Chinese style was peculiar to Worcester, but that this is not so is proved by the recent discovery of a piece [10], now in the Burn Collection, which is certainly not Worcester but which shows the use of black outline and enamel washes to perfection. The decoration consists of a typical Chinese landscape, with trellised fence, trees, water, rocks, and island with pagoda. In the foreground is a seated boy with a bird perched upon his hand. The foliage is washed in with an extremely transparent green, a lifeless, slatey blue gives colour to the water and to the pagoda roofs, and the rocks and the costume of the boy have touches of a muddy, opaque brown. We are not unduly concerned here with questions of provenance, but a distinct kinship with a great deal of Longton Hall porcelain is obvious.

Although there is a superficial resemblance between black printing and black pencilling it is not difficult to differentiate between the two. The free, boldly drawn strokes of a brush are thicker than the deliberate cuts of the graving tool, and they possess immeasurably greater and obvious spontaneity. Nevertheless, just as the Chinese sometimes copied underglaze blue-printed decoration in brushwork, so English artists have been known to make careful copies of black-printed designs, whose rarity merits careful watch being kept for them.

Kakiemon Patterns

In a preceding chapter mention was made of the 17th-century Japanese potter, Kakiemon, who introduced the particular style of pattern which has taken his name, and which was admirably suited to the seeming fragility of much Japanese ware. It is necessary to add somewhat to what has already been said about the origins of the many English copies, and to clarify the rather misleading names which have been given to them. Kakiemon worked at Arita, and the Arita wares were exported from Imari, so that all three names have been applied indiscriminately to patterns having a Japanese origin. For our present purpose the name of Kakiemon is most fitting and 'Imari' will be used to describe the later and more decadent styles which have inspired such patterns as 'Derby Japan', 'Spode Japan', 'Old Japan', 'Old Imari', and so on.

True Kakiemon ware seems to have been made between 1650 and 1720, but very little of it, for a reason which has a strong significance where decoration is concerned. Chinese porcelain-making was state controlled and somewhat regimented, which resulted in a certain formality and monotony. Decorators worked to rule, as we have seen, whereas the Japanese, at least in the days before they were bitten by the export bug, were bound by no such restrictions. It follows that an artist such as Kakiemon was at once draughtsman and colourist, and his output was therefore comparatively small. This meant that Japanese originals were infrequently available to English decorators, who had perforce to copy from Chinese or Meissen versions of them which often lacked the true Kakiemon features, which are as follows:

1) Line drawing was not used as a guide for the enamels, but rather as an intrinsic part of the decoration; the artist painted in the manner of a water-colourist, in washes, and used line only when necessary.

2) The use of underglaze-blue was exceptional, a brilliant but opaque enamel taking its place. Chinese copyists used the underglaze-blue, and reserved their enamel for '*famille verte*' decoration.

3) The other colours used were transparent yellow, blue-green and yellow-green, a great deal of red (especially in borders), and gold. Aubergine was occasionally used, but more usually on Japanese 'Kutani' (or 'Kaga') wares.

4) Designs consist for the most part of a central motif of flower sprays, animals, fishes, a figure, or birds beside a flowering shrub or perched upon a tree, with a narrow floral or simple diaper border. Chinese motifs were occasionally used, but on the whole Kakiemon and his school chose designs based on a definite native school of painting known by the name of Tosa.

Such was the true Kakiemon, which should not be confused with the later wares which were made in response to European demands. In these inferior developments the lack of individualism is immediately apparent, the blue enamel is replaced by underglaze blue which was applied as a careless background for comparatively un-skilled brushwork, and the lovely red enamel became muddy and unattractive. This sort of decoration would not have been adopted if it had not been fully acceptable to the Western market, and it set the standard for much tasteless early 19th century decoration in 'Japan' styles.

The finest Kakiemons were made at Bow, where the management evidently appreciated the suitability of their simple colourfulness for domestic wares. Frequent mention is made of them in John Bowcocke's papers (now in the British Museum), of '8 dozen mosaic plates', for instance (mosaic being another name for diaper), and of the well-known 'wheatsheaf' pattern [1] – 'has Mrs Bernardeau had what she ordered of the Wheatsheaf?' Again, it is evident from the Sales Catalogues of 1757, 1758, and 1764 that Kakiemon wares were held in high regard, for there are references such as the following – 'a large assortment of fine enamel and fine Partridge sets, which are

[1] *Bow Porcelain*, Hurlbutt, pl 24.

most beautifully painted by several of the finest masters from Dresden', 'fine desserts of the fine old Partridge and Wheatsheaf patterns', 'large table services of the finest Old Japan patterns' and, perhaps most significant of all, 'some part of this porcelain is very little inferior to the fine old brown-edged Japan, and wants no other recommendation than its beauty and service.' The 'wheatsheaf' was one of those painted by the 'masters from Dresden', about 1765, and it follows that the design was a Meissen adaptation, featuring birds of the earlier and less flamboyant 'exotic' variety, one of which is perched on a flowering tree beneath which is the familiar banded hedge or 'wheat-sheaf'. The enamels are green, yellow, blue, and red in two shades, the usual Kakiemon palette, but the tightly packed, red, floral scroll border [11] owes nothing to the original. This same pattern, in slightly different styles, was copied at Worcester, Chelsea, Derby, Plymouth, and Bristol – it is the most common of all, and other factories [12] used the wheatsheaf motif as the basis of their own designs.[1] The composition of the 'partridge' pattern [11] is similar, equally well balanced, but with a pair of partridges or quails feeding under the rather fantastic, gnarled tree.[2] The same colours were used, although the blue enamel of the earlier examples of about 1755 was opaque and inclined to be milky, whereas by about 1760 it had become darker and more transparent. This pattern also was extensively copied, at Worcester the fine honey gilding was sometimes replaced by brown enamel, and the birds less skilfully drawn. It was used at Chelsea, and at Longton Hall, very little changed from the Meissen original except for slightly different treatment of the tree and of the herbage at its roots.

The 'Cock' pattern mentioned by Bowcocke is quite different.[3] Mr Hurlbutt described it as painted in the Imari manner, by which we understand that although the direct inspiration was Chinese it was yet Kakiemon at second hand. It is interesting to notice that the bright, garlanded border which encloses the pair of lively, furious fighting cocks (which were originally phoenixes), is much more intricate and ambitious than those of the floral scroll type, and formed the basis of the festoons which reached perfection on Bristol porcelain. We should not, finally, leave the Bow Kakiemons without mentioning the strange rarity of specimens which must have been made in very large quantities, some of them being used for the quite enormous services which were then customary. Of the rarer patterns only a handful survives, so rare as to be unnamed, but possessing in common the same economy of colour and the same delicate use of Japanese motifs.

At Chelsea there was another range of patterns in addition to those which were

[1]Frank Lloyd Collection, pl 16, no 82. [2]*Ibid*, pl 8, no 50; *Bow Porcelain*, Hurlbutt, pl 23. [3]*Ibid*, pl 25.

borrowed from Bow; [1] the 1755 and 1756 Catalogues list the 'tyger and wheatsheaf', 'tyger and rock', and 'Hob in the Well' [2] which, as Mr Honey tells us, was the name of a popular play of the times, misapplied to the Japanese design illustrating the story of a boy who saved his companion's life by smashing the water-jar into which he had fallen. The dates of the catalogues make it clear that such patterns are found on pieces of the red anchor period. The finest of all Chelsea Kakiemons is a picture of two birds with outspread, flowing tail plumage, the one perched upon a delicately drawn tree, the other flying threateningly above. [3] Similar birds are to be seen in one of the few Chelsea blue-and-white patterns and, in colours, and in a similar pattern, on Worcester specimens. [4] Yet another pleasing pattern of quite a different sort was used mainly for octagonal pieces, for which its alternating radiating panels of concentric scrollwork and small floral motifs are admittedly well suited. [5]

Kakiemon patterns, of whatever factory, are characterized by the effective use of a simple colour scheme, by their similarity to the originals (particularly at Bow), and by their delicacy, which is so well suited to the seeming fragility of the early fritt porcelains.

Japan Patterns

There is such a great difference between the Kakiemons and the patterns commonly known as Japans that the latter must be discussed separately, although both had a common Japanese (or Chinese) origin, and are often classed together for that reason. The explanation of the difference between them cannot be too strongly stressed or too often repeated, because it provides a ready means of division. The Japanese, because of European demand, gave up the reticence of the Kakiemon school in favour of intricate patterns based upon the 'mosaic' of their silk brocades and lacquer work, which was painted on the later, coarser ware. This sort of decoration was usually aesthetically inferior, but the earliest examples of the 1760s, as copied at Worcester, are nevertheless extremely decorative. Just as the Kakiemons were painted best at Bow, so at Worcester the Japans were almost an exclusive speciality, whether they were exact copies from Japan, China, or Meissen, or whether they were imaginary creations with something in them of all three. They saw nothing incongruous in the blending of Meissen flowers, mosaics, or scale pattern, Japanese diaper, and Chinese *famille verte* shagreen, and the blending was done cleverly. Thus, when the Worcester catalogues listed their Japan patterns in 1769, many of them which have

[1] English Ceramic Circle Exhibition Catalogue, 1948, pl 45, nos 208, 210, 216.
[2] *Ibid*, pl 46, no 222. [3] [4] Frank Lloyd Collection, pl 18.
[5] Schreiber Collection, pl 26, no 130.

since been identified prove to be hybrids, yet possessing in common a distinctly Oriental look despite their cosmopolitan origins. Here are some of them – 'fine old Japan star pattern', 'Japan pattern flowers', 'Japan Sprig pattern', 'old scrole Japan', 'old Japan fan pattern', and, of course, the Kakiemons.

Before attempting to envisage the more splendid patterns which were the highlights of Worcester decoration from about 1765 to 1770, we ought to consider for a while those which were used for the less costly wares, the 'bread and butter' patterns which were easy to produce in large quantities and which had in common certain simple motifs. Of these the 'Old Japan Fan'[1] is the most familiar, consisting of fan-shaped panels of radiating 'petals' in underglaze blue, red, and green diapered with gold, circular gold-diapered blue medallions, and an underglaze blue border with a floral scroll reserved in white, which is a typical feature of many Worcester Japans. Then there is the considerable class of patterns in which panels radiate from a central circular panel [18 & 22] in which a single chrysanthemum head is painted,[2] or more rarely a spray of flowers, or branches of flowering shrub; the panels are painted alternatively with diaper of various patterns, flowers, dragons, or other Oriental emblems. A common feature is the placing of a chrysanthemum head in the middle of a gold-diapered panel, and the wheatsheaf motif is often included in floral ones. The 'old mosaic Japan'[3] belongs to this class, with its eight radiating panels, four of them diapered, one of gold flowers on a blue ground, and three of flowers painted in enamels. In this and in many other patterns the formal lines of the panels are broken by the scattering of several large flower heads upon them. An unusual feature of this intricate and lovely Japan is its extensive colour scheme, which includes turquoise, yellow, and pink in addition to the usual underglaze blue, red, and green. Yet another colour, aubergine, was sometimes used, and on a well-known pattern of eight alternating panels of diaper and flowers a soft Indian red effectively replaces the more usual crimson as the basic ground colour. These were the patterns which inspired the Japans of the early 19th century, because they were comparatively easy to paint, could be produced quickly, and yet were satisfying to those who demanded plenty of gay colour on their domestic wares.

The more ornate Worcester Japans exist for the most part as specimens in well-known collections, splendidly decorated vases, bowls, and mugs, and it is clearly impossible to do more than to indicate the nature of their decoration, especially as so many of them fall more easily into later chapters. The scale grounds in blue and pink, for instance, were frequently used as the groundwork for large panels of fanciful birds, flowers, fantastic dragons, and insects. On other pieces the same motifs, always

[1]Frank Lloyd Collection, pl 10, no 60. [2]*Ibid*, pl 11, no 63. [3]*Ibid*, pl 10, no 58.

brilliantly enamelled, are to be seen reserved upon plain ground colours, upon gold-netted or diapered ones, or upon the '*famille verte*' shagreen or dotted green. A typical example is a vase in the 'fine old Pheasant pattern', in the Dyson Perrins Collection,[1] a wonderful example of rich and careful painting, with upright panels in which are pheasant-like birds on a twisted tree, separated by bands of flowered trellis on a deep blue ground. Around the neck is a vermiculated red band, interrupted by panels of flowers, and with all this magnificence there is still the simple border of white floral scrollwork reserved on an underglaze blue ground. The 'old Dragon Japan' is similar,[2] but the 'pheasants' have given place to a winged dragon, a gracefully curling beast, beside a flowering shrub.

The fashion changed at Worcester when Japans gave pride of place to the sumptuous styles of Meissen and Sèvres, to the 'exotic birds', flowers, and landscapes, to the coloured grounds and to the scaled ones. At the same time the Japanese influence began to be felt elsewhere, for it is then that we find free copies of the brocaded 'export Japanese' patterns on Chelsea-Derby wares, very tasteful ones, reticent in contrast to the luxurious styles which the Chelsea painters had taken with them to Worcester. No 4 in the still existing Derby pattern book is a typical example,[3] painted in the usual Japanese colours of blue, red, and gold with four radiating panels of diaper on which lobed, oval panels of stylized flowers are reserved. Unfortunately, the attempts made by Bloor to revive the fortunes of the factory resulted in the 'Derby Japans'. In 1817 he advertised for 'twenty good painters' of Japans, and that they were forthcoming is proved by an outpouring of patterns which are meaningless, crowded, and incredibly garish, although, of course, they served as admirable cover for some of the imperfect ware which had to be painted and sold as part of the recovery plan. It is ironical to realize that although perfection was reached at Derby in so many other decorative spheres, yet such patterns as these spring automatically to mind whenever the name of the factory is mentioned. It is a bad chapter, and would be better forgotten, were not its effects so widespread. In the first place, the rivalry between Worcester and Derby, never quite dormant within the past two hundred years, was awakened into keen competition when it became apparent that Bloor's efforts were successful. Worcester had no need to invent, but only to revive, and the old patterns were given a new lease of life, particularly at the Chamberlain factory. Some were re-introduced practically unchanged, others were made more splendid, but always they retained some of their old character, and never descended to the low Derby level. It must be confessed, also, that the Worcester patrons had become a little weary of the

1 *Worcester Porcelain*, Hobson, pl XLII, fig 2. 2 *Ibid*, pl XLII, fig 3.
3 *Crown Derby Porcelain*, Gilhespy, pl 61, fig 108.

classic shapes of the first few years of the 19th century, with their impeccable ground colours and careful painting of landscapes, flowers, and figure subjects. Even the Prince Regent gave an order in 1811 for a 'Harlequin' set, in which every piece was painted with a different Japan pattern, and the vogue lasted until about 1820.

By this time the pioneer factories were rivalled by many younger but flourishing concerns, and the Potteries were eager and able to keep in step with Worcester and Derby. At Stoke-upon-Trent Spode fell wholeheartedly into the spirit of the times, and 'Spode Japans' quickly became popular. Let it be said, to begin with, that the Spode decoration usually achieved splendour without vulgarity, even though their creations were almost entirely the products of their designers' fertile imaginations. 'The productions of Minton, Spode, and Daniell were really elegant, and evinced quite as much skill in their manufacture, if not ornamented in so costly a manner.' Thus said R. W. Binns, historian of the Worcester factory, and his last phrase was a greater compliment than he perhaps intended. Even before Japans became so very popular, as early as 1803, Josiah Spode experimented with hybrid patterns in the Oriental style [19, 20], as, for example, the well-known no 967,[1] with its zig-zag fence and flowering shrubs in blue, green, red, pink, and gold, a pattern which though colourful and gay, and admittedly geometrical, is more akin to the reticent Kakiemon than to the ornate Derby Japan. Throughout their development the Spode Japans, whether they were factory inventions or whether, more rarely, they were inspired by specially obtained Japanese originals, always possessed the same tastefulness and showed the same careful thought to the permissible ratio of painting to white body, and it is, of course, wrong to suppose that Josiah would have been so unwise as to copy the Derby patterns which he aimed successfully to rival. Indeed, the pattern books and the many existing specimens tell quite a different story, particularly as regards a class of Japan which Spodes made their very own by the use of the single colour, red, in conjunction with gold, a class approached only by Flights in their occasional copies of Kutani wares for sheer brilliance and good design.

It might seem that undue stress has been laid upon a single one of the Staffordshire factories, to the exclusion of others which were flourishing at the same time, but the scope is clearly too wide to do otherwise. We should find, if we looked deeper, that the Japans of others were copies or variations of the styles of those who set the fashion. We should find that a great deal of fine work was done at Mintons and at Davenports, and at many other smaller places which are overshadowed in retrospect by the larger concerns. Nevertheless, brief mention should be made of just one other factory, if only because it shares with Plymouth and Bristol the distinction of having made English

[1] *Spode and his Successors*, Hayden, facing p 118.

44

'true porcelain'. There is still considerable mystery about the actual arrangement which led to the founding of the New Hall pottery at Shelton, but it seems probable that its life lasted from 1782 until 1825, during which time true porcelain was made until about 1810, to be followed by bone porcelain. New Hall decoration is very similar to that which is seen on Bristol of the 'cottage' type or, in later years, on the wares of contemporary Staffordshire factories. Very occasionally, however, a little more initiative was shown, and in this regard there is an important class of Japans painted in blue, red, and gold which are outstanding for their restrained design, and which are unlike those of any other factory [17].

'Famille verte' and 'famille rose'

The finest Oriental 'famille verte' porcelains were made during the K'hang H'si period (1662–1722), and they were so jealously prized that pieces were not readily available as copies. For this reason the characteristic, bold, flowing brushwork, with the predominant green enamel, underglaze blue, Indian red, pale yellow, and manganese purple, and the rich brocaded borders are rarely seen on the early fritt porcelains. Later, when the K'hien Lung artists had perfected the 'famille rose' pinks and carmines of the preceding Yung Cheng period, export from China had become more usual, and there was no lack of specimens from which to copy the characteristic raised, opaque enamels and, on occasion, the equally characteristic elaborate and often minute brushwork.

When designs in 'famille verte' style are seen at all on our native porcelain, one can say broadly speaking that they are seen on Worcester specimens,[1] though even then they are seldom true copies, because alien colours were introduced into the original palette. On the whole, too, the Oriental accent on green is usually absent, not so much because there is less of it, but because the imitation is so much less lustrous and vivid than the original. The so-called 'Bishop Sumner' pattern[2] is an excellent example of a fairly true translation, featuring a central medallion with landscape, kylin, and phoenix, with six radiating panels containing rocks, flowers, birds, and fantastic monsters, and with a narrow floral border. The name is difficult to understand, because no bishop of that name was alive when the pattern was introduced about 1770. Since there were later Bishops Sumner, both of Winchester and of Canterbury, it is probable that later ownership gave a name to the pattern, as has so often happened. The 'Kylin' pattern is very similar,[3] but includes additional colours; the central medallion is painted with a

[1] *Worcester Porcelain*, Barrett, pls 1, 4*b*, 5, 6*b*, 8*a*, and 10*a* and *b*.
[2] Frank Lloyd Collection, pl 1, no 2. [3] *Ibid*, pl 2, no 3.

rosette, from which radiate either four or eight panels, alternatively containing monsters and tables with vases of flowers. The green is provided by the dotted brocade pattern which separates the panels from the hexagon cell border, whereas in the 'Bishop Sumner' version it is properly a part of the painting of the motifs. The same factory produced many lovely copies of the much prized Chinese combinations of powder-blue and panels of 'famille verte' decoration, featuring birds on flowering boughs, vases and emblems, sprays of flowers, and landscapes.

The later years at Worcester saw little attempt to continue or to revive the early designs. The 'Kylin' pattern was used for services, both at Flights [16] and at Chamberlains, and the latter produced a rather crowded and anglicized version of it, featuring a round central medallion containing a monster, and four heart-shaped ones with monsters and tables with flowers, all reserved on the familiar dotted green ground. The space between the reserves is filled with butterflies and flower sprays, in enamels completely alien to the traditional palette, and contrasting violently with the otherwise Oriental appearance of the pattern.

Just as Worcester was the home of the 'famille verte' copies, comparatively few though they were, so was the 'famille rose' adapted widely at Bow,[1] and clearly at an early date, for the famous inkstands bearing the words 'New Canton' are sometimes dated 1750 or 1751 and are painted in this style.[2] The general colour scheme is admittedly feminine compared with the virility of the earlier 'famille verte', for its rose-pinks, carmines, pale green and aubergine, and white have a common, rather weak tone value. Nevertheless, they tone admirably with the early creamy paste, and with the applied white sprigs of prunus which often accompany enamelled decoration.[3] The range of motifs is limited – tree-peony, the chrysanthemum, insects, pheasants, rocks, and bamboo – and the treatment is usually summary, with little attempt to imitate the detail of Chinese specimens. At Chelsea use was made of the same colour scheme, though Chinese models were not as a rule exactly copied. It was the basis also of the mandarin decoration of Worcester and other factories, where we have seen that the treatment was frequently detailed in the true style of the 'ruby-backed' Oriental.

It is natural to expect that the true aesthetic value of the two restricted palettes would not be understood in later years, for with increased facility in colour making their intrinsic economy was ignored, and painting grew ever more naturalistic. Mention has been made of the decoration upon the stone china of Spodes, and on this same body we find outstanding work in the colours of the two families. Much the same can be said of the stone china of Mintons, Mason, and Davenport, for it was left

[1]Herbert Allen Collection, pl 7, no 23. [2]*Bow Porcelain*, Hurlbutt, pl 2a and b. [3]*Ibid*, pl 13a.

to them to carry on the early traditions while the porcelain makers travelled on to explore fresh sources of design.

Miscellaneous Styles

The range of Oriental decoration is so wide that there are many styles which do not fall readily into any of the classes discussed. Consider, for instance, those patterns which 'look like Chinese' and yet had no true Chinese or Japanese origin, such as the well-known 'Whorl' pattern[1] of Worcester, Caughley, Lowestoft, and Derby. It has been given other names – 'Queen Charlotte', 'Catherine Wheel', 'Queen's', and 'Spiral' – and it consists of either vertical or spiral panels, alternatively red on white and white on blue, with or without gilding. Where the pattern originated is not known, the only certain fact being that the only known Chinese examples are later in date than the English ones, and were probably copied from them. It should be noted that the Derby blue is a mazarine, whereas at the other factories indigo was preferred.

A most popular class of decoration has for many years been referred to as 'Chinese Lowestoft', a name which is at once both paradoxical and significant. There is no need here to stress the truth that such ware is purely Chinese in origin, made at Canton for export to Europe, in that sense the name is misleading and inaccurate. On the other hand, there is little doubt that much of the decoration upon it has definite kinship with that seen upon fritt-paste Lowestoft, despite the seeming improbability of Chinese artists having imitated the wares of such an insignificant factory. The likeness lies in a partiality for line-shaded pink roses, and figures in mandarin style, for ribbons and designs of flowers and rocks similar to those used in the 'Redgrave' pattern,[2] in red, blue, and green, or in red and blue alone. Sometimes further ornament was introduced in the shape of applied thin rolls of white clay, and always there was the frequent incorporation of armorial bearings, sketches of which were, of course, sent out to China when services were ordered. When it was within the powers of the English factories to supply similar wares, magnificent heraldic painting was done, and this must form the subject of a separate chapter.

Such were the styles which have so immeasurably enriched our native porcelains. The difficulty of defining their attraction, to which we referred at the beginning of this chapter, is not eased by any sort of description; the collector of Chinese porcelain will always scorn its English imitations, no matter how well copied they may be, and there is deeper reason for his preference than mere superiority of paste or colour. If one

[1]Schreiber Collection, pl 62, no 579. [2]Herbert Allen Collection, pl 85, no 492.

might hazard an explanation it would be that the fascination of the Orient which inspired the early designers of furniture and ceramics has never been entirely conquered by Western civilization. A 'mandarin pattern' on a modern plate is still as strange and exotic to us as it was to the artist who painstakingly copied it on an early piece of Bow, Chelsea, or Worcester.

CHAPTER SIX

Ground Colours

The transfer of interest from paste to decoration is almost complete when full use has been made of ground colours, since their colourfulness must attract to the near exclusion of other virtues. Almost, but not quite, for the beauty of a colour is to a large extent dependent on the body beneath it, as may be realized when comparing, for instance, the behaviour of enamels upon the *pâte tendre* of Sèvres and upon the 'hard' paste which followed it. Furthermore, the customary reserving of white panels as canvases for fine decoration, particularly against dark grounds, added the necessary contrasting relief which enhances any painting, and which is essential if it is to be seen to the best advantage.

We must first remember that the third quarter of the 18th century saw a progressive increase in the amount of decoration done outside the factory. Even such an established concern as Coalport availed itself of the services of the London decorating establishments, whose artists painted not only their specialized subjects but also, sometimes, the ground colours accompanying them. Naturally enough, as the years passed, the larger factories gathered together their own staffs of capable artists, and formed their own pattern books, while some of them, such as Worcester and Spode, were self-contained from the very beginning. Nevertheless, when we consider the colours and styles of any particular factory we must not lose sight of the possibility that their similarity to those of another may have this logical explanation.

There are two ground colours which were in common use from the beginning, and which have already been discussed – powder-blue and ordinary underglaze blue. We have seen that the former was used with underglaze blue painting and, later, as a background for panels of polychrome painting,[1] while the latter often formed a groundwork for gold ornament or else served as part of the scheme of a Japan pattern. Such decoration as this was entirely in keeping with the early emphasis on Oriental styles, but other coloured grounds for the most part owed their origin to Meissen, where practically every known early English colour had been used before 1750, and whence they reached this country either direct or by way of Sèvres. It is interesting

[1]*Worcester Porcelain*, Hobson, pl XXXVIII.

49

in this regard to appreciate the fact that both French and English imitations were superior to the German originals, because of the extreme 'hardness' of the Meissen paste. In the same way, though in reverse, when the Sèvres authorities changed their paste there was an immediate deterioration, with a need to discard certain colours and to invent new ones.

The numerous Sèvres enamels have already been described, most of which were copied in this country at various times and with varying success, notably at Chelsea. Consider first the rare and lovely crimson which is nowadays usually known as 'claret'. The Yung Cheng decorators of the early 18th century were probably its inventors, and Böttger certainly introduced a pink enamel before his death in 1719, from which a ground colour was evolved. Then, at Sèvres, a comparable pigment was introduced, the '*Rose Pompadour*' which was imitated at the London factory and which was at first given the same name, since the Catalogue of 16th February 1770 mentions 'fine Pompadour dishes and compotiers'. Later in the century the word 'claret' was substituted, but by whatever name it is called the Chelsea colour, though varying in tone as a result of technical difficulties, could on special occasion possess an evenness of warmth and colour seldom equalled by any other factory. This extremely rich pigment [1] is probably one of those referred to as early as 1760, when the Sale Advertisement praised 'some new Colours which have been found this year by Mr Sprimont, the proprietor, at very large Expence (sic), incredible Labour, and close Application'. Mr Sprimont was proud of his new colours, and certainly his crimson is seen to advantage as a foil to beautifully painted '*chinoiseries*' in the style of Herold of Meissen, and to copies of the work of such as Lancret, Teniers, Boucher, and Watteau. Judging by its popularity another Chelsea success was the dark blue which was the splendour of the gold anchor period, and which was known either as '*Mazaren*' or '*gros bleu*'. We read of it first, by name at any rate, in the 1756 Catalogue, and again in 1763 as the 'most rare and truly inimitable Mazarine blue and gold.' [2] This lustrous and glowing underglaze colour does indeed show at its loveliest when it has gilding upon it, either in the form of tracery, or thickly encrusted flower or bird painting, for its depth and strength demand that sort of lighter relief. Chelsea used a yellow ground, [3] but it would seem that it was copied direct from Meissen rather than from the Sèvres *jaune jonquille*, if we may judge by the sorts of painted subjects usually found with it [30]. [4] We speak to-day of a lovely restful green as 'apple-green'. This was the pea-green of Chelsea, and it dates back to 1759, but its heyday had not yet come and, like tur-

[1]Schreiber Collection, pl 28, no 215. [2]*Old English Porcelain*, Honey, pls 15 and 16.
[3]*Cheyne Book of Pottery and Porcelain*, pl 21, no 52.
[4]Figures within brackets refer to plates at the back of this book.

quoise [32, 34], it is rare on Chelsea porcelain, though not so rare as a ground colour of pure gold,[1] which was entirely a Chelsea speciality.

When Duesbury took over the factory certain changes took place, in keeping with his commercial outlook and acumen. The use of turquoise and crimson was extended, because he gave the necessary study to their cheaper production, and greater use was made of gold in such patterns as the 'gold stripes',[2] which was copied from Frankenthal, and which is a groundwork made up of concentric or radial stripes on which figures or landscapes were painted in oval medallions. Establishment at Derby brought with it more changes and additions, the dark mazarine was gradually replaced by a brighter lapis-lazuli in imitation of the Sèvres *bleu-du-roi*, an enamel colour which was called 'Derby Blue' or 'Smith's Blue' [81],[3] while a canary yellow and a pleasing mauve were also entirely new. At the same time, the migration of the Chelsea painters to Worcester rather than to Derby is clearly betrayed by a retrogression which Duesbury was powerless to prevent, and Derby ground colours, though used in greater abundance, lack the pulsating depth of the Chelsea ones. The last decade of the century brought with it a range of new colours, including pale pink, lavender, pale yellow, fawn, pale red, and a gold pattern copied from Sèvres, known as 'seaweed'. Exactly similar ones were used at other contemporary factories, as we shall see, for the days of 'mysteries' were of the past.

Since the Chelsea painters went to Worcester about 1768 it is that factory which should now logically be considered, though of course they merely augmented an already proficient decorating staff which had brought the unique scale grounds to perfection. It is idle to attempt to trace the origin of this most famous of all ground patterns because versions of it are to be found on wares of many nations and of many periods. It is only certain that scale pattern in blue, crimson,[4] pink,[5] yellow,[6] brick-red,[7] and pink 'peacock'[8] was used at Worcester before 1760, and that both the blue and the pink are common on the sort of Chinese porcelain which was copied there at that time. The basic colour of the commonest scale, the blue, was the underglaze *gros-bleu* which was mentioned in the 'mazarines' of the factory sales catalogues, darker and more inclined to indigo than its Sèvres namesake, very like the Chelsea mazarine when it was thinly applied, but inclined otherwise to be opaque. The pattern was made in two ways, for at first each scale was clearly outlined, darkly, with the brush, whereas later it was found easier to wipe out the centres, giving a rather smudgy

---

[1]British Museum, no II 95. [2]*Crown Derby Porcelain*, Gilhespy, pl 15, fig 25.
[3]*Ibid*, Pl 1; Schreiber Collection, pl 45, no 387. [4]Schreiber Collection, pl 63, no 541.
[5]*Worcester Porcelain*, Hobson, pl LXXXIX. [6]Frank Lloyd Collection, no 148. [7]*Ibid*, no 29.
[8]Herbert Allen Collection, pl 21, no 93.

scale which was at the same time somewhat smaller. The popularity and worth of the scale patterns has attracted the attentions of the forger, but his scales were (and still are) commonly transferred, as are those of modern factory replicas. The date of the intro- duction of the overglaze pink scale is hinted at by a piece dated 1761, in the Dyson Perrins Collection, and this colour is extremely rare, as indeed are the red and yellow varieties. All four, nevertheless, have in common their use on the very finest speci- mens, in which the painted decoration is reserved in rococo heart-shaped or scalloped panels, heavily edged with the finest honey gilding in all sorts of scrollwork. The most common sort of decoration is the 'exotic bird' in its many different varieties,[1] sometimes with insects or flowers, followed in order of rarity by flowers, 'chinoiseries' in the style of Pillement,[2] and figure subjects in Watteau style.[3]

Closely akin to the scaled grounds, at least in general appearance, are those in plain mazarine[4] or powder-blue, on which much the same sort of reserved decoration is painted. Instead of the relief afforded by the pattern of the scales we find all sorts of gold enrichment, diaper, traceries,[5] and floral motifs, just as was done at Sèvres and Chelsea, the breaking up of a rather overpowering colour by the delicately applied gilding. The white panels left uncovered against the powder blue are usually of the same shapes as those seen upon ordinary 'blue-and-white' wares, fan-shaped and round, which is natural when we consider that the blue was applied before final decoration was decided, and the brighter appearance of polychrome specimens, and their more finished neatness, is entirely due to the gold which tidies up the edges.

The Worcester proprietors lost little time in taking full advantage of the influx of the Chelsea workers, for in the *Public Advertiser* of 5th May 1769, they extolled their mazarine and gold, sky-blue, pea-green,[6] French green, sea-green, purple, and scarlet, 'enamelled in the highest taste and curiously painted in Figures, Birds, Land- scapes, Flowers, Fruits, etc.' For the most part the Worcester ground colours rank among the finest ever made, sometimes equalling those of Sèvres and surpassing some of those of Chelsea, though the mazarine and claret were never brought to quite the same perfection. The development of an extensive range of colours led to a decline in the popularity of the scale patterns, the blue variety in particular being replaced by the thick, opaque, pea-green enamel [67, 87, 103] which we now call apple-green,[7] the most like to Sèvres of the entire range. It was perhaps realized that green showed to much better advantage by artificial light than blue, which tends to appear as purple

[1] *Worcester Porcelain*, Hobson, pl xcii. [2] Frank Lloyd Collection, pl 6, nos 29 and 31.
[3] *Worcester Porcelain*, Hobson, pl lxxxv. [4] English Ceramic Circle Exhibition Catalogue, 1948, no 422.
[5] Frank Lloyd Collection, pl 18, no 84. [6] *Ibid*, pl 19, nos 94 and 95.
[7] *Worcester Porcelain*, Hobson, pl lxx.

under a light of any strength. A peculiarity of the apple-green was its inability to take gilding upon its surface, so that the usual scrolled edging had to be applied to the un-covered, glazed paste. Another colour which gained in popularity over the mazarine was the *bleu celeste* mentioned in the sale catalogues, a very clear and distinctive turquoise enamel, while the lapis-lazuli, though having the appearance of an enamel was in reality an underglaze blue of bright and vivid tone. Claret was rarely success-ful, [1] for besides being very expensive to produce, its colour was uncertain, inclined to pink, and far removed from the true Chelsea crimson. A very pale yellow was often used effectively with flower painting in Meissen style, or with panels of Oriental land-scape in crimson monochrome, with Kakiemon border and scattered flower-sprays[25]. This yellow ground is known upon a mug which bears a silhouette portrait of Dr Wall and the date 1761, but it should be recognized that later wares similarly coloured may well have been decorated outside the factory, judging by the styles of decoration upon them. The Orientally inspired 'shagreen' [66] and 'dotted green' continued in common use, usually in Japan patterns, [2] but also as an alternative to blue or scale blue grounds, and the Chelsea 'gold stripes' was occasionally copied. [3] In this regard it is well to remember that factories of importance were often asked to make and to paint replacements for services made elsewhere, a practice which resulted in out-of-period decoration.

The later Worcester factories, especially the two larger ones, seem to have had little difficulty in making whatever colours they desired, though the 'harder' pastes they had developed resulted in tones less rich than those of the earlier pigments. The mazarine blue and the crimson were still popular, the former being used mostly for reproductions of the early styles of flower painting [72], with deep borders heavily gilded, and the Japan patterns continued to make use of underglaze blue as part of their colour scheme. Mazarine was used in a new way, as a foil to the best work of the specialist painters; it was applied in narrow borders upon which running geometrical or foliate ornament was painted in gold [118]. The Chamberlain mazarine is particu-larly fine, deep and attractively uneven in tone, whereas that of Flights and of Graingers tends to be flat, and is more usually seen with patterned gold upon it. Chamberlains introduced a matt cobalt which is extremely pure and even, unvarying in colour, and at its best when thick, tooled gold scrolling compasses the panels of painting contrasted upon it [69, 128]. The range of greens is endless, from a rank-looking blue-green (introduced by Flights in imitation of a characteristic colour used

[1] *Worcester Porcelain*, Hobson, pl LX; Frank Lloyd Collection, pl 34, no 166.
[2] *Worcester Porcelain*, Hobson, frontispiece.
[3] Frank Lloyd Collection, pl 13, no 110; Schreiber Collection, pl 64, no 580.

by Pratts on their colour-printed earthenware), to a very lovely yellow-green used at the same factory. Common to both we find pale pink, rich salmon, numerous maroons, peach [71], and clear ivory. Vermilion, though overpowering, was sometimes used at Chamberlains to good effect.

Considerable use was made of broken grounds, of the 'sea-weed' [75] and vermiculated in particular, both upon white and coloured backgrounds, either combined with painting or as decoration in itself, and a new departure was the introduction of painting to imitate marble which was entirely in keeping with the classical taste of the period.

The concentration upon the early use of ground colours was restricted almost wholly to Chelsea and Worcester, the other contemporary factories probably having neither the facilities nor the staff to enable them to compete. Thus, at Lowestoft, a very immature, smudgy blue scale seems to have been the height of attainment apart from ordinary powder blue, and at Bow the situation was much the same, with an occasional copy of Worcester scale blue [1] or of Chelsea mazarine. [2] Only at Longton Hall was an entirely original and worthwhile colour perfected, a striking blue known as 'Littler's Blue'. William Littler used it first upon his earlier earthenware body, upon which it shows dully, but on porcelain the effect is entirely different, because the whiteness beneath gleams unevenly through and imparts vitality to it, with a mottled or streaky effect rather like that seen in the Worcester mazarine, but more pronounced. It is commonly supposed that the pigment was applied with a sponge, but it is also quite obvious that the colour was prone to run excessively in the kiln. Littler used it to fill moulded panels, on alternate overlapping moulded leaves, with unfired size gilding, traces of which are now seldom seen, or more rarely as a ground colour for reserves of painting. [3]

The developments described in connexion with Worcester are fairly representative of those throughout the industry, but there are occasional tours-de-force to the credit of others. The short-lived Pinxton concern (1796–1813) developed a very fine yellow, [4] a pinkish fawn, and a range of greens which have a natural kinship with those of Derby. At Rockingham (1820–42) the typical landscapes and flowers were painted in panels reserved on grounds of *gros-bleu* (thick, deep, and often inclined to violet), green (yellowish, and extremely opaque), magenta, neutral grey [52, 82], bright Reckitts Blue, and a yellow inclined to buff. The Nantgarw colours, notably turquoise, scarlet, deep blue, [5] *Rose Pompadour*, [6] lavender, and green, [7] were often

[1]British Museum, no 1, 40. [2]Schreiber Collection, no 105.
[3]*European Ceramic Art*, vol 1, Honey, pl 172a. [4]*Old English Porcelain*, Honey, pl 84b.
[5]*Nantgarw Porcelain*, John, pl 52a, b, and c. [6]*Ibid*, pl 50a and b. [7]*Ibid*, pl 13a and b.

good enough to pass as genuine Sèvres, but it is safe to say that most of them were the work of London studios. The use of *'oeil de perdrix'* tracery in gold and in colours was common,[1] particularly on the deep blue, and there was an entirely new and successful green, a rich olive-green known as *'vert foncée'* which was used mainly for borders, broken by oblong floral reserves.

The Great Exhibition of 1851 was the occasion for a wonderful array of porcelain decorated in styles old and new. Some of it was garish and impossibly ostentatious, for the period was not remarkable for its good taste in art, but there is no doubt that an exception must be made in the case of Coalport porcelain painted in the French style. The 'Sèvres Revival' at Coalport was a belated attempt to imitate the best of the *'vieux Sèvres'*, for though at Coalport, as at other factories, tentative attempts had always been made to copy and to rival the husks, festoons, urns, and figure subjects of the French factory, it was not until the period 1830–60 that its greatest glory, the fullest use of ground colours, was successfully rivalled on a large scale. There can be no doubt that the Coalport productions were good enough to pass as the real thing, even when the forged Sèvres mark was not placed upon them by unscrupulous London dealers or, even, by the factory itself.[2]

The imitation of these ground colours called for considerable re-invention on the part of Rose's workmen, and we are on fairly sure ground in tracing the inception of some of the more splendid and successful ones. The maroon probably came first, and it is supposed to have been the invention of Billingsley's son-in-law, Samuel Walker, well before 1830. The turquoise was more difficult, for the first expensive attempts produced only the pale pink colour called *'celeste'*, to be followed by the perfected tone about 1850. The same approximate date holds good for a new deep underglaze blue which was the Coalport version of the French *bleu-du-roi*,[3] and for the loveliest colour of all, the *Rose Pompadour*.[4] At its best this was equally as soft, rich, and opaque as the Sèvres original, and the ultimate development of the earlier but less perfect 'Venus Pink'. Other Coalport ground colours include a variety of buffs, greens (including an apple-green equal to that of the earlier Worcester, but scarcely as opaque) [36, 38,] orange-red,[5] canary yellow, and brown.

The name of Thomas Martin Randall cannot be disassociated from any mention of Salopian porcelain making and decoration. He learnt his trade at Caughley, whence he travelled to Derby, Pinxton, and London, where he worked as an outside decorator. Finally, about 1825, he founded his own small pottery at Madeley, which is near Coalport. Here he continued not only to paint on white Sèvres porcelain, but also

[1]*Nantgarw Porcelain*, pl 22. [2]Barrett, figs 160–2. [3]*Idem*, figs 128 and 129. [4]*Idem*, figs 126, 127, and 131. [5]*Idem*, fig 136.

to manufacture a lovely fritt paste body which is almost indistinguishable from the Sèvres *pâte tendre*. Randall's ground colours, as might be expected from a painter of his long experience, are exceptionally fine, in particular a deep blue enamel [97] to which gold diaper was usually added,[1] and a lovely turquoise like that of Coalport. The fact that Madeley porcelain was made until 1840 would seem to indicate that a considerable amount of it still awaits identification.

Finally, in the Potteries, the porcelain makers were not idle. Spodes' felspar body proved to be an admirable base for new colours of good quality, particularly a very unusual deep, rich fawn. This colour is unpopular nowadays for a reason already touched upon; it was intended to be seen by candlelight, and modern electric lighting makes it drab and lifeless. Other Spode colours were pinkish-grey, pale green [126], canary yellow, and pale biscuit; these are the successful ones, for the matt blue is far inferior to that of the Chamberlains, the lavender [100] lacks clarity and looks uneven and dirty, and the dark blue is usually inclined to purple. Strangely enough, the popular turquoise was but rarely used, and was left to the rival Minton firm to perfect [98], and to use to full advantage on the Parian wares.

Apart from the intrinsic beauty of a good ground colour, whether used by itself or as part of a design, no other sort of decoration is quite so interesting if the trouble is taken to study its origins from the very beginning. The collector of Chinese monochromes has to look back to the Sung dynasty to understand the significance of many of his coloured glazes and enamels, and there is deep interest even in the chemical reasons for their innumerable varieties and tones. The lover of English porcelain, likewise, will do well to learn a little about the practical potter's skill in this regard. In doing so he will not only the better appreciate his apple-green, his clarets, and his blues, but will at the same time find it easier to identify and date his pieces.

[1] Barrett, fig 160.

CHAPTER SEVEN

Flower and Fruit Painting

Flower painting stands high in favour as a decoration on porcelain, for the very nature of a flower, with its fragility, its freshness, and its colour, seems to make it so admirable a subject to be represented upon a substance which itself is fragile and which has a certain indefinable freshness of its own, and which yet demands colour to enhance its beauty. The same remarks apply to fruit, though to a lesser degree, for it is an old axiom in any sort of painting that colours which are found together in nature will never clash.

We have already seen that flowers were used as decoration on the first fritt porcelains, copied either from the Oriental or from Meissen. But although painters of the old school, whether upon canvas or ceramics, were wont to depict everything as it really looked, to give a true and recognizable likeness rather than an impression, they did not often copy direct from nature, but more usually from the work of others before them. The result was that the first period of flower painting, up to the end of the 18th century, tended towards conventionality, as we see for instance on Japan patterns or on copies of the *famille rose*. The second phase was well begun by such as Billingsley and Pegg, who copied from nature or from books on botany, and whose flowers and fruit were naturalistic. Then came a reaction, for in the 1830s Edwin Steele of Derby founded a school of formal representation, the stereotyped school of Rockingham, Davenport, Coalport, and later Worcester, which was finally, but only temporarily ousted by a style of painting, not only of flowers but also of landscapes, in which a rather cloudy, 'open-air' effect was obtained. This style is seen at its best on Doulton and Worcester wares of the late 19th century. All four styles are equally decorative, but it is to be expected that naturalistic flowers, considered in their own right as works of art, are held highest in repute.

Flower and fruit painting is so individualistic that it is only possible here to attempt a broad generalization of styles, whereas it is obvious that each effort of each of the innumerable painters ought to be studied separately. This is not possible, and the reader must examine many actual specimens, or illustrations of them in specialist monographs, to supplement our remarks here. So much depends on the colours of a palette and on their exact tones, and every artist had his own peculiarities of drawing,

57

his favourite subjects, and his characteristic pigments. Beginning arbitrarily enough with Bow, we find the early use of the prunus blossom and peony in the '*famille rose*' style,[1] a form of decoration which is effective rather for its soft colourings and good arrangement than for its botanical accuracy. The Oriental influence then gave way to the French, which made itself felt in the pretty 'Bow Flowers' in their close bunches, with large central blooms and projecting sprigs of smaller ones. This is a remarkably soft and delicate style peculiar to the factory,[2] though the influence came probably from Mennecy, and pieces so treated can be dated about 1755. The last ten years brought another imitated style, but this time from Chelsea, which lacked the reticence and delicacy of the Bow Flowers but which was made effective by the use of bold, strong colour.[3] In most respects Bow is a mysterious factory, and there is little evidence apart from the wares themselves upon which theories may be based, and much the same is true of Chelsea, which claims next attention. The triangle marked specimens of the period 1745–50 were painted with two sorts of flowers, either in small detached sprays with insects, attractive in their simplicity and practically effective in hiding the blemishes of the early body, or, more rarely, by rather laboured 'Meissen Flowers' [28][4] whose popularity lasted well into the red anchor years.

The Chelsea Sale Catalogues spoke of 'Indian Plants', by which they almost certainly meant the '*Indianische Blumen*' of early Meissen which had been adapted from the Oriental. These rather exotic flowers, with their vaguely tropical appearance, are typical of the painting of the 1750s.[5] More rarely the deservedly famous work of the Chelsea 'Fable Painter' is sometimes accompanied by flower sprays by another hand. The third class of Chelsea flower painting constitutes the initial use of the botanical style which was later developed at Derby, and it is well known that the wanderings of those who had served their apprenticeship there resulted in a widespread adoption of the Derby style. In this way a much later cult of flower painting may be said to have had its beginnings in the free, bold brushwork of the Chelsea men, whose lovely colours allied to well-balanced composition make their work so attractive.[6] Broadly speaking, the Chelsea botanical painting may be separated into two classes which have been aptly named 'Hans Sloane' and 'Naturalistic'. In 1760 the curator of the famous Hans Sloane gardens, Philip Miller by name, published two volumes of engravings of 'useful and uncommon plants', and it is clear that many examples of Chelsea flower painting were copied from them. As is usually the case

[1]Schreiber Collection, pl 9, no 38. [2]*Ibid*, pl 10, no 73; *Old English Porcelain*, Honey, pls 27*a* and 28*d*.
[3]Schreiber Collection, nos 76 and 103.
[4]Figures within brackets refer to plates at the back of this book.
[5]*Old English Porcelain*, Honey, pl 7*c*. [6]*Ibid*, pl 7*a*.

when flowers are copied from engravings the Hans Sloane flowers have a stiff pain-staking appearance, and are sometimes notable more for their curious 'uncommon' nature than for their beauty [29]. The 'naturalistic' flowers have in common with later Derby work the fact that they were almost certainly painted from nature. Dr Mackenna has concluded that all were painted by the same hand, probably only on pieces of the raised anchor period, and that the same artist was responsible for the flowers on the fable-decorated pieces. These flowers, and the insects and butterflies which often accompany them, are outstanding for attention to detail, even to the reproduction of blemishes in leaves or blooms; the brushwork is delicate yet free and bold, and the colours very true to nature. The gold anchor period was more notable for beautifully painted but extravagant versions of old styles than for new introductions, in keeping with the emphasis on splendour rather than simplicity, and emphasizing the change in fashion which demanded magnificence as a thing in itself.

The Worcester decorators of the matured years excelled in flower painting, as they did in decoration of every sort. Binns speaks of 'quaint posies of old-fashioned flowers' and enumerates many which were commonly represented, among them the rose, chrysanthemum, carnation, blue nemophila, and auricola. As usual the earliest attempts were in the Oriental style, but in the form of 'Japans' instead of the versions of the 'famille rose' preferred at Bow. Such flowers are quite impossible but nevertheless decorative, often betraying a crudeness of execution which characterizes much of the work done before the invasion of the Chelsea painters in the late 1760s. This is not to say that accomplished painting was never done before their time, as we may see from some of the Meissen inspired flowers, rendered in fresh colours and individually treated, [1] while also belonging to the early years are the exquisite flowers bordering the figure subjects of the 'Fable Painter'.

The Meissen flowers and fruits, it has been well said, ripened at Chelsea but were harvested at Worcester. There are the small bouquets and scattered sprigs [62], the so-called 'Deutschen Blumen', rendered in naturalistic style, and the bouquets of idealized flowers, the 'Meissner Blumen', with their accompanying groups of sliced or whole fruits and vegetables. [2] The many painters had their diverse styles. One, whose work is well known although he is nameless, favoured large, sprawling sprays which covered the entire surface, [3] and another, by way of contrast, arranged a single large flower in the centre of a single bouquet, with tiny sprigs projecting from it. [4] Sometimes flowers were thrown in festoons across the reserved panels, [5] or arranged

[1] Old English Porcelain, Honey, pl 64a. [2] Worcester Porcelain, Hobson, pl LXIX, no 1. [3] Frank Lloyd Collection, pl 31, no 141. [4] Ibid, pl 33, no 152. [5] Worcester Porcelain, Hobson, pl LXIX, no 2.

diagonally from corner to corner, but always the colours are soft and blending, a feature which places the Worcester work in a class by itself. Furthermore, it is note-worthy that in other classes of painting colours are apt to be much more garish, as in many of the 'exotic bird' compositions.

Whether naturalistic or stylized, formal or pretty, the flower painting which was reserved in finely gilded panels against scale or plain grounds [65] is the most pleasing of all the styles of decoration of the fine middle period. Gradually, as the influence of Chelsea was felt, flowers by themselves were augmented by fruit, birds, and insects, and amongst those who excelled in flower and fruit painting was one whose style is seen on many Worcester specimens. He had a liking for a fig with calix, for well-rounded, 'spotted' fruits, pea-pods, sliced fruit, filbert nuts, berries, and radishes, and for a tulip with a single projecting petal. Examples of his work, and of pupils who worked in his style, may be seen in many collections, and Mr Hobson proved that he must have come to Worcester from Meissen, by way of Chelsea, since his brushwork is found on the porcelain of all three places. [1] Another painter preferred large, beauti-fully drawn fruits, sometimes spotted, accompanied by insects. [2]

The Sèvres influence brought with it comparatively few new ways of painting flowers, inasmuch as their use was principally incidental in such patterns as the well-known 'trellis' or 'hop-pole' variations which were copied so successfully. [3] We see them mainly as festoons and garlands, usually without stems or branches, carefully and minutely drawn but somewhat insignificant, although an occasional fine render-ing of 'French Flowers', as they were called, betrays the work of one who was clearly not an ordinary piece worker. [4] The most reticent of all the French styles features dainty floral sprays, festoons, and bouquets painted in dry overglaze blue or pink enamels, enriched with equally delicate gilt scrollwork. [5]

Later Worcester flower painting, as seen on the porcelain of Chamberlains, Flights, and Graingers, is almost entirely of a naturalistic nature, and is for the most part in-distinguishable from contemporary work at Derby, Coalport, Swansea, and Spode, to mention but a few of the factories where floral decoration was predominant. It is an unfortunate fact, furthermore, that all records of the Worcester workmen were destroyed by fire, and as nothing was signed any sort of classification by painters' names is at the moment out of the question. It is clear only that there was sufficient co-operation between the factories to allow of considerable movement of employees

[1]Frank Lloyd Collection, pl 22, no 118; *Worcester Porcelain*, Hobson, pl LVIII.
[2]Frank Lloyd Collection, pl 22, no 119. [3]*Ibid*, pls 37 and 38; Schreiber Collection, pl. 57, no 544.
[4]*Old English Porcelain*, Honey, pl 75*b* and *c*.
[5]Schreiber Collection, pl 57, no 606; Frank Lloyd Collection, pl 27, no 126.

between them. Certainly, apart from the remarkable depth, detail, and good colour of much of the Chamberlain painting there is little to choose between the styles of the three concerns – in the light of what has just been said this is only to be expected – and it is perhaps well to observe that the painting of roses on Graingers porcelain is fully equal to that of its more flourishing neighbours. We shall not stress here the possible handiwork of the formidable Billingsley, for although it is probable that he would have painted at least a few pieces during his stay in Worcester, his real employment both at Chamberlains and at Flights was in a technical capacity. Among lesser mortals the Flights artist, Moses Webster, stands high, and we shall hear of him again at Derby, where a colleague wrote of him:

'If Moses composes his posies of roses,
   Of sweeter he can't them compose.'

Binns says of him that his flowers were of a 'somewhat dashed and faded appearance, as if they had been kept in water too long', and that 'his groups are tastefully arranged and there is a dash and freedom in his execution'. Thomas Baxter painted first at Flights and later, after a three year visit to Swansea, at Chamberlains. He is best known for fine, detailed figure painting, which is readily identifiable, but he also painted flowers. It is probable that his style in this regard was based rather on impressionism than on accuracy, his tightly packed bouquets will not bear close scrutiny, and the same may be said of the work of Lowe, one of his pupils, who later set up a decorating establishment in the city. Lowe's bouquets usually centre around a pair of roses placed back to back, the petals ill-defined and scattered. Other recorded Flights painters were Samuel Astles, a skilled hand at botanical flowers remarkable for their detail,[1] Stinton, famous for 'flowers and flies'[2] (and not to be confused with his later namesake of 'Highland Cattle' fame), Thomas Crowther, and Richards. Many masterpieces of fruit painting may be studied on Chamberlains porcelain, for which a painter named Steel was probably responsible.

In every branch of decoration the two larger concerns attempted frequent revivals of the older styles – indeed, this is even now a feature of the work of their modern successor – and the Chamberlain attempts to rival some of the more decorative ones were usually successful, notably in the use of a particularly intense, dark underglaze-blue, which had panels of naturalistic bouquets or sprigs reserved upon it, or else was used as a border to such central bouquets as the star-shaped one which was a feature of the 1770s [72]. The Flights, being apparently more enterprising, rarely copied exactly, and Graingers used flowers in unusual and attractive ways, so that we may

[1]Worcester Museum Works Collection Catalogue, no 1166. [2]*Ibid*, no 1170.

find a single, well-painted rose thrown carelessly upon a gold 'sea-weed' pattern [75], or a botanical spray in conjunction with unconnected scrolled gilding.

We should now retrace our steps to consider the painting done by the contemporaries of the early factories at Bow, Chelsea, and Worcester which laid the foundations for the later work which has been described, for all had their contribution to make towards the predominant early 19th century styles. William Littler's difficulties at Longton Hall in making any sort of serviceable porcelain prevented him from making full use of the experience which he must have gained during his salt-glaze years. The flower painting on his porcelain is little different from the earliest Worcester attempts, we find the same bouquets and sprigs with an extensive use of pink roses, but with petals tremulously though clearly outlined [47], and with a frequent use of a peculiar and unmistakable yellowish-green enamel, often together with a bright pink outlining of leaf edges and veins.[1] The Lowestoft painters gave to the same sort of elementary decoration[2] a typical immature and unskilled appearance; it is rare to find any degree of proficiency, and the curious custom of shading pink rose petals with nearly parallel lines[3] has been partly to blame for the perpetuation of the 'Chinese Lowestoft' myth, since much export Chinese porcelain was painted in just the same way. Indeed, there is very little Lowestoft decoration which does not show an obvious Oriental influence, and we may class as flower painting such designs as the 'Redgrave' pattern, with its conventional rocks and flowering peonies in opaque, bright blue and red, sometimes accompanied by a rank-looking, sticky green.

It cannot be too strongly stressed that much exceptionally fine painting was done at Liverpool. The *Williamson's Liverpool Advertiser* for 4th December 1761 had an advertisement for the Sale by Auction of some of the wares of one of the many factories, Reid's China Manufactory. In this sale was included 'enamelled Coffee cups from 6/- to 2/- a dozen, and all sorts of china cheap in proportion.' The cheapness is undeniable, but what of the enamelling at such a price? For the most part it would be in floral or 'Mandarin' style. Had we been present we should have expected to see a rather impressionist sort of painting, with free brush-strokes, and with leaves washed in green over crude black outline. Petals would be blobs, and so would the darker centres of the spherical roses forming the centres of the bouquets. We should have seen frequent use of a bluish violet and a rather cold, flat crimson.[4] Above all, we should have said to each other that this was something like Worcester, not so good, but what can you expect at the price?

In a previous chapter we spoke of the 'blue-and-white' decoration on Caughley

[1]*Old English Porcelain*, Honey, pl 48*a* and *b*. [2]Schreiber Collection, pl 55, no 455.
[3]*Old English Porcelain*, Honey, pls 53 and 54. [4]*Ibid*, pl 79; V. and A. Museum, no C1186-1924.

porcelain, and, of course, it is for that sort of decoration that the factory is best known. At the same time, partly because of this emphasis on blue painting and printing, and partly because few have troubled to look beyond it, other styles of Salopian painting have been ignored or else placed to the credit of others. Actually, apart from occasional shading of rose petals, there is little resemblance between Caughley painting and that of Lowestoft, with which it is often confused, for the former is usually careful, often laborious, even if the blooms themselves look more artificial than real. A sepia enamel which was commonly used for leaves,[1] veined with gold, is quite alien to Lowestoft, though it was sometimes used at Worcester, and so is the typical close bunching of the bouquets,[2] which are painted in pink, yellow, purple, puce, and 'dry blue'. The rather dull sepia is sometimes omitted with brightening effect. So far as polychrome flower painting is concerned, Turner's visit to the French factories resulted in little save the adoption of slight sprig patterns such as the 'Bourbon Sprig',[3] on domestic wares, and the use of 'dry blue' festoons, bouquets, and sprigs which may equally well have been copied from Worcester.

It is now time to talk about Derby, a factory which shares with Worcester the boast of a well-nigh unbroken history from the beginnings to the present day. Of those beginnings there is little enough to record apart from what has already been said about the Chelsea styles, which Duesbury continued after the amalgamation. Thus, in the Chelsea-Derby period of 1770–84 we find little that is new, for the Sèvres style still persisted, though the swags and the festoons, and the detached sprays were treated with a refinement and delicacy which presaged the future, and the painting of flowers in green monochrome was a related and very beautiful innovation. Previous to this are the flowers of which Mr Honey speaks, with the thread-like stalks,[4] and the well-balanced, open bouquets which might well have been painted at Worcester, though indeed this factory would have added the borders which its decorators liked, but which the Derby specimens do not commonly possess.[5]

Collectors of Derby are fortunate in that so many of the painters are known by name. One of the earliest was Edward Withers, who was at Derby from the beginning until about 1790. He was before the time of the naturalistic style, and his work was intrinsically conventional. He outlined his petals and his leaves (the latter in black, grey, or brown, washed in with the old copper green, in two shades), and left his highlights white in the old-fashioned water-colour style. Indeed, Withers' flower subjects have much of the charm of contemporary drawings in that medium, they are always graceful and attractive, with petals few and clearly drawn, especially on roses, and

[1]Barrett, figs 62 and 63. [2]*Idem*, fig 65; *Old English Porcelain*, Honey, pl 83b. [3]Barrett, fig 69. [4]*Old English Porcelain*, Honey, pl 38a. [5]*Ibid*, pl 41d.

63

often with a single, curved spray springing from a bouquet in a manner reminiscent of a later artist at Chamberlains.[1] One of Withers' known contemporaries was a Frenchman who may have been brought to Chelsea by Sprimont, George Complin by name, who worked at Derby roughly between 1758 and 1795. His style was very like that of Withers, but his colours were altogether more gay, occasionally unnatural, but nevertheless attractive. Sometimes he painted fruit, accompanied by small animals or birds with no attempt at correct proportion, so that several writers have spoken of a 'squirrel as small as a mouse'.[2]

William Duesbury, as his account books clearly reveal, was himself a skilled enameller, and he chose his artists with discrimination. Thus, although the famed Crown Derby period of 1790 to 1800 saw the production of large quantities of domestic ware painted with sprigs, sprays, and garlands, more and more porcelain was painted by a growing band of experts, of whom the most outstanding was William Billingsley. This well-known figure was apprenticed at Derby in 1774, and when he left in 1796 it was to the evident despair of his employers, for it is recorded that it was said at the time that 'his going into another factory will put them into the way of doing flowers in the same way, which they are at present ignorant of'. This prophecy came true, for his naturalistic style was adopted wherever he went, and it was spread further by the wanderings of his many pupils. There is little doubt that so long as Withers worked in the factory Billingsley's genius was wastefully employed in the copying of standard factory designs, so that his fully matured work is to be seen only on pieces made between 1790 and 1796. It is, I think, a mistake to attempt to identify it by means of pattern numbers or painters' numbers – of the latter the 7 commonly attributed to him is also to be found on pieces obviously painted by others, and although there are ten numbers in the pattern books marked to be done by 'Billensley', the same patterns were almost certainly in use both before and after his employment. What then are the characteristics of his style? In the first place, and in the nature of a warning, it should be said that examples of his brushwork are incredibly rare, though those of his imitators and pupils are numberless. The only true guide is for the student or collector to examine and to learn an undisputed specimen, whether of Derby, Nantgarw, or Swansea. It is a style which at all events stands supreme by reason of sure, free drawing, excellent composition and perspective and, therefore, a lifelike appearance which tempts the admirer to pick the flowers from off the piece. Billingsley's roses are rounded, yet they are slightly dishevelled, and do not possess the compactness of, say, a wax imitation. Above all, the highlights are wiped out, leaving behind a faint tinge

[1]*Derby Porcelain*, Hurlbutt, pls 23 and 24; Schreiber Collection, pl 47, no 408; British Museum, no III, 18.
[2]*Crown Derby Porcelain*, Gilhespy, figs 54 and 55.

of colour. Add to this the fact that his green was commonly of the opaque variety, sometimes tinted with a little orange-brown, and verbal description can convey little more. [1]

When Billingsley left Derby it was necessary to find a competent successor, and the choice fell on William Pegg, or 'Quaker Pegg', as he is often called. Pegg must have been a strange character, and a source of constant anxiety to his superiors, for his strong religious convictions were ever in conflict with his art. 'Thou shalt not make unto thyself' was always at the back of his mind, and his frequent periods of remorse deprived the factory of his services for months at a time, his longest absence lasting from 1801 to 1813, when he was persuaded to return until his final retirement in 1823. Pegg's speciality was the painting of life-size flowers [42–44] botanically accurate, which usually spread over the whole surface of the porcelain. His famous moss rose omits no detail, [2] for each hair is separately drawn. So careful was he to ensure that his accuracy should be recognized that it was his habit to write the names of the flowers making up a bouquet separately, in red, on the underside of the piece. Like Billingsley, Pegg used chrome green, a yellowish shade in contrast with the old translucent, brighter copper green, through which the outline and veining of a leaf would show. A further aid to identification was put forward by Mr Hurlbutt, who suggested that Pegg was allowed to mark his own pieces with the crown and batons mark unusually wide and flattened. [3]

There has been much controversy concerning the alleged decline in every branch of decoration during the Bloor proprietorship of the first half of the 19th century. Emphasis was undoubtedly placed rather on quantity than on quality, but the flower painting probably suffered least from the lapses in taste which sometimes affected other styles of decoration. Briefly, naturalism was discarded for a mannerized style, a flatter and less realistic manner of painting which was probably introduced by the younger Steeles. The father, Thomas, was a disciple of Billingsley and so painted in his manner, [4] but his sons, Horatio and Edwin, found it easier, one suspects, to develop a hard and facile way of drawing, with a conventional palette which included (to quote Mr Honey) 'a sharp pink, a foxy red, and a deep orange.' Edwin took his

[1] Derby Porcelain, Hurlbutt, pls 19 and 20; Ceramics of Swansea and Nantgarw, Turner, pl XXXII; Crown Derby Porcelain, Gilhespy, figs 47 and 49; Herbert Allen Collection, nos 135 and 166; English Porcelain Circle, Transactions, 1929, pl. XVI; V. and A. Museum, nos 3046–1901, C175–1910, 1–1873.
[2] Derby Porcelain, Hurlbutt, pls 21 and 22.
[3] Crown Derby Porcelain, Gilhespy, Figs 57a and 58; V. & A. Museum, 3068–1901; Connoisseur, vol X (1904), p 190.
[4] Herbert Allen Collection, pl 37, no 152; Old English Porcelain, Honey, pl 46c; Derby Porcelain, Hurlbutt, pl 50; Crown Derby Porcelain, Gilhespy, figs 91 and 92; V. & A. Museum, 3036–1901.

mannerisms with him to Bristol, and his brother took his long-stemmed blooms and love for vetches to the Potteries. It is interesting to note that painting in his style is to be seen on much Chamberlains porcelain, but it is not known whether he ever worked at Worcester. Thomas earned from Haslem, who was a good judge, the tribute that 'as a painter of fruit on china he had no superior, if indeed he had any equal in his day.' His colours are rich and harmonious, with well-balanced grouping and an attractive absence of hard edges. His fruits are rounded, taking reflected light from each other, and naturally stippled by means of a dabbing on of colour with the finger tip to the still wet ground colour. [1]

We have spoken already of Moses Webster, of his dashed and faded flowers ('crushed-hat roses', Mr Rackham calls them), freely executed and tastefully arranged, [2] and he did this sort of work at Derby from 1816 to 1825. Leonard Lead was an imitator of the Steele brothers, a lover of startling colour contrasts and smoothly curving sprays. [3] Edward Hopkinson's clear-cut outlines belong to the same school, and Haslem praises the 'agreeable freshness and look of nature' [4] of another contemporary, Cuthbert Lawton, who together with John Keys carried Billingsley's style into the later times when more florid decoration was preferred.

Billingsley himself took his innovations and characteristic methods to many places. From Pinxton, where he was the arcanist rather than the artist, between 1796 and 1801, we have a few specimens which are plainly from his brush or perhaps from that of a pupil, [5] but for the most part decoration consisted of landscapes, although we cannot omit mention of a variety of sprig patterns such as the 'Paris Cornflower' in blue, green, and pink, [6] which are found upon fluted tea-wares similar to those made at Derby, Caughley, and Worcester. Billingsley worked at Swansea from 1814 to 1816, broken by a brief stay at Nantgarw, but as at Pinxton he was mainly concerned with the attempted introduction of his lovely paste and glazes, and very little decoration can be definitely attributed to him. It is known, nevertheless, that he taught painting at Swansea, and made a series of designs which was the basis of the Swansea school of flower painting. [7] David Evans and Henry Morris were probably two of his pupils, the former noted for his garden and wild flowers and for his strawberries, [8] and the latter for his tightly bunched bouquets, painted in brighter colours. [9] After Billingsley's departure William Pollard was responsible for the finest painting, and his wild

[1]Herbert Allen Collection, pl 40, no 193. [2]*Derby Porcelain*, Hurlbutt, pls 25 and 26.
[3]*Crown Derby Porcelain*, Gilhespy, fig 87; Herbert Allen Collection, nos 179 and 194.
[4]*Crown Derby Porcelain*, Gilhespy, fig 73. [5]*Schreiber Collection*, pl 91, no 796.
[6]V. & A. Museum, no 3081–1901.
[7]*Swansea and Nantgarw Potteries*, Meager, pl vi, no 29, pl vii, nos 50 and 73, pl viii, no 334, pl ix no 53.
[8]*Ibid*, pls x, xi, xii, no 74, xv, no 308. [9]*Ibid*, pl xiii, no 72; *Old English Porcelain*, Honey, pl 86a.

flowers and fruit, in peculiarly soft and delicate colours, are outstandingly lovely [56, 57]. They were invariably loosely bunched, and it was his custom to fill the spaces between them with a rather indefinite purplish-black.[1] Thomas Baxter [58] was in Wales only for three years, between 1816 and 1819, where he painted botanical flowers.[2]

Outside decorators were responsible for the greater part of Nantgarw porcelain painting. Among them was John Sims, formerly of Derby, who worked in London from about 1805 to 1821, and who was noted for his large, somewhat indeterminate open roses. A fellow Derby painter, James Turner, worked for him, and painted clusters of three roses, back to back in trefoil shape, with projecting trefoil leaf sprays.[3] Moses Webster ended his working career with Robins and Randall, and his work there is often seen on Nantgarw pieces.[4] Among the factory decorators was Thomas Pardoe, 1821 to 1822, whose style is so like that of Billingsley as to account for many pieces supposed to have been painted by him. It seems that everything came alike to this most prolific artist, for we see his hand on quite ordinary wares as well as on important pieces, in styles ranging from sketchily drawn sprays and isolated flowers to 'wetly' rendered large mass groupings. His favourite flowers were large, open, pink roses, multi-petalled, and tulips in full bloom with drooping outer petals, painted in deep purple on bright yellow. He often omitted the stems of smaller blooms, and his leaves may either be of ordinary elm shape or like maple leaves, with regular pairs of balanced veining. Like Pegg, Pardoe sometimes named his flowers, but in separate letters, whereas the former inscribed his in a flowing hand.[5] Thomas had a son, William Henry, who specialized in designs of conventional flowers and leaves in small yellow urns, or in brightly painted bouquets which are commonly seen on chocolate-edged plates. William Weston Young sometimes put his hand to decoration, for he was a water-colourist of local fame. His work is amateurish, at any rate as regards flower painting, for his blooms are stiff and laboriously correct, probably because in common with others, but lacking their interpretative skill, he copied from Curtis's *Botanical Magazine*.

The excellence of much Coalport flower painting[6] has undoubtedly led to much Salopian porcelain being placed in Swansea cabinets, as Mr Honey was the first to point out. A wave of enthusiasm for this branch of decoration began at the factory about 1815, coinciding with a remarkable extension of the available palette, and we

[1]*Old English Porcelain*, Honey, pl 86b; *19th Century English Pottery and Porcelain*, Bemrose, pl 59B.
[2]V. & A. Museum, no 3491–1901; *19th Century English Pottery and Porcelain*, Bemrose, pl 54A and B.
[3]*Nantgarw Porcelain*, John, pls 11b and 29b. [4]*Ibid*, pls 26a and 31a; *Old English Porcelain*, Honey, pl 85b.
[5]*Nantgarw Porcelain*, John, pls 46 and 49c. [6]Barrett, figs 90 and 91.

find that the Pattern Books list no fewer than twenty-one colours which were new factory inventions. The same books, wonderfully coloured, reveal the names of many painters, who were supported for less important or repetitive work by a staff of women – the words 'Flowers by Girls' and 'Women's Flowers' are repeatedly seen. The chief artist during the first period, the 'Revived Rococo' as it has been called, seems to have been named Kelshall, for his name constantly occurs in connexion with loose, trailing patterns, long, thread-like stalks, and fruiting branches. J. Birbeck specialized in roses and fruit, Thomas Dixon in bi-coloured pansies and Passion Flowers, Cecil Jones in botanical painting in the style of Pegg, and H. Stephens in baskets of flowers and Sèvres motifs. Despite the fact that many skilled artists were available, however, it is noticeable that pink or purple outlines were often used for the guidance of the artists, who were thus disciplined by the restrictions of the pattern books.

After 1830 came the revival of the Sèvres styles, which resulted in the remarkably fine Coalport ground colours, but which had little effect on flower painting. William Cook painted flowers and fruit in the French style [38] – he probably copied direct from Sèvres porcelain – using emerald green shaded with bright orange for his foliage, and favouring circular clusters of tiny flowers with the spaces between them filled in with harmonizing colour.[1] Cook later went to join Randall at Madeley, where he painted on Sèvres and Madeley porcelain. Many fine plaques belong to this same period, similar to those made at Derby, which were produced as show pieces and which were painted at Coalport by Jabez Aston and R. Eaton.[2]

It is almost impossible to identify unmarked early 19th century porcelain, because so many artists carried the lessons of their training to so many other factories. Thomas Steele, for instance, went from Derby to Davenport, so that we find there a purely Derby naturalistic style, with richly gilt borders.[3] Edwin went to Rockingham, and his hand is seen on ornamental pieces with landscapes by another artist.[4] Other recorded names are Brentnall, Llandig, and Collinson, but nothing is known about their styles. But above all it was in the Staffordshire potteries, apart from those places already mentioned, that the naturalistic style flourished, even though it was a style shared by all and differing only in degree of excellence. At Mintons the resumption of porcelain making about 1825 saw a distinctive method of bold gilding on coloured grounds, with reserved panels of crude, hotly painted flowers;[5] Bloor's unsatis-

[1] *Barrett*, fig 131. [2] Herbert Allen Collection, nos 403 and 626; Barrett, fig 149.
[3] *19th Century English Pottery and Porcelain*, Bemrose, pls 58a and 70; V. & A. Museum, nos 2550–1910, c289–1914.
[4] Herbert Allen Collection, nos 596, 598, and 601; *Old English Porcelain*, Honey, pl 96; V. & A. Museum, no 47–1869. [5] Herbert Allen Collection, pl 90, no 517.

factory management drove many Derby painters into the Potteries, and Hancock and Bancroft found their way to Mintons. Spodes, with their instinct for popular taste, seized greedily upon the Derby decline, and their glorious flower painting was eagerly bought by the post-Waterloo *nouveaux riches*. Josiah's artists produced very fair imitations of the Billingsley roses, even to the typical 'wet' brushwork, they reserved bouquets against scale and plain grounds of every conceivable colour [53, 54], alternated flowers in white relief with gaily painted sprays, and surrounded bouquets with heavily gilded borders. Like Rose, of Coalport, he developed the use of transfer outline, but on a much larger scale. Many colours were used, including blue, black, and brown, on specimen pieces and on services alike, and the printed outlines served as the foundations for innumerable different colour schemes. [1]

There yet remains the flower painting of the late 18th century 'hard paste' factories at Plymouth, Bristol, and New Hall, whose alien porcelains place them in a class by themselves. Cookworthy's wares, made at Plymouth and Bristol, bear several different sorts of decoration. Copies of the 'India Flowers' were painted in crude red, yellow, and copper green,[2] sometimes with the addition of blue and gold,[3] semi-natural flowers were well arranged in crescent-shaped sprigs, and painted in several yellows, opaque green, and dirty blues,[4] and, finest of all, the Meissen style was copied, with detached sprigs in greater detail and with the use of a fuller palette. For those responsible for this work the reader is referred to the writings of Owen (pp 289 and 299), Jewitt (vol I, p 397) and Pountney (p 224), but it is difficult definitely to identify the work of any particular artist. Flower painting continued to be the predominant form of decoration on the Bristol porcelain made by Champion, and under his direction was developed the style which is always considered to be typical of the factory, consisting of festoons hanging from gold rosettes or from ribbons, or intertwined with gold lines,[5] sometimes of equal lengths and sometimes alternatively long and short. The flowers are usually naturalistic, well arranged, and include tulips, martagon lilies, nasturtiums, poppies, convolvulus, and roses. Colours are invariably clear and bright, with good pinks, translucent yellows, strong reds, and bright leaf-green. Dr Severne Mackenna's researches have led to the conclusion that the best of this work was done by William Stephens, whose hand is sometimes betrayed by his rendering of initials in tiny pink flowers and gold foliage, or in gold alone (*Apollo*, August and September 1953). Many services in this style were made for Champion's friends, and a full list of them can be found in the Catalogue of the Trapnell Collec-

[1] *Spode and his Successors*, Hayden, facing pp 74, 78, 80, 82, 84, 86.
[2] *Cookworthy's Plymouth and Bristol Porcelain*, Mackenna, fig 32. [3] *Ibid*, pl 6. [4] *Ibid*, pl 2.
[5] *Champion's Bristol Porcelain*, Mackenna, fig 70.

tion, pp. XXII to XXVII. Other Bristol styles include botanical work very like that of Derby, though more delicately done, [1] and some lovely bouquets in harmonizing colours. [2] Much Bristol decoration resembles that of Chamberlains, for the juxtaposition of bluish and yellowish greens is common to the foliage of both, though the Bristol laurel wreaths are not commonly found on Worcester wares.

If it is certainly true that the secrets of the Bristol concern were sold to the New Hall combine, there is no doubt that the ability to carry out the same sort of decoration was entirely lacking in the artists of the new factory. The 'hard paste' which was at first continued certainly bears the sprigs and festoons, but they are gloomily painted in black, pink, and red; the Bristol carefulness of brushwork is seldom approached and is replaced by an immaturity comparable with that of Lowestoft, whose decoration is indeed somewhat similar in style. The later bone-ash paste commonly bears decoration which is in no way different from that of many other Staffordshire factories. It is rather a sad thought that two factories which we tend to think of as the last survivors of the smaller concerns should end on an undistinguished note. Their closure marked the beginning of a new era in which the success of a factory depended upon the comparative skill of its artists.

[1]*Champion's Bristol Porcelain*, Mackenna, fig 49. [2]*Ibid*, fig 2.; Schreiber Collection, pl 86, no 735.

CHAPTER EIGHT

Landscape Painting

Landscape is not commonly found on English porcelain made before the end of the 18th century, if by landscape we mean the purely English style which was developed to such a high level at Derby and, to a lesser degree, at Worcester. There are naturally early exceptions, at any rate as regards technical excellence, at Chelsea and Worcester, but for various reasons the early factories fought shy of landscapes, and the best contemporary work was done by outside establishments. In the first place, it is true to say that landscape painting demands a high degree of skill which was possessed by few of the factory artists. Broadly speaking they were copiers of foreign styles which lost little from a decorative point of view even if they were somewhat distorted in the copying, provided that they adequately filled the given space and combined good 'balance' with harmonious colours. But landscape was a different matter, calling for knowledge and skill possessed only by those factory hands, few in number, whose work comprises the rarities, and by those who gravitated naturally to specialist decorating establishments by reason of their exceptional ability. Whether a landscape is painted upon canvas or upon porcelain, it must from the public point of view 'bear looking into', mere copying seldom gives a natural result, and nothing is more difficult than to paint realistic sky, water, and foliage. Later on, as proficient artists not only practised themselves but also founded their own schools of painting, the position was changed, and natural inclination to paint a good landscape was further encouraged by those who were eager to have their homes and estates painted upon porcelain, and by employers who saw subtle advertisement in the custom. It must be obvious, of course, that the rendering of elaborate scenery on porcelain cannot be considered as art of the highest standard. Indeed, its practice is really all part and parcel of the decadence which is so often apparent during the first half of the 19th century, at a time when the cry was ever for more colour, more gilding, more extravagant shapes. In submitting to it the pottery owners had an outlook very different from that of the painter on canvas, who will often starve rather than pander to a fashion he knows to be vulgar or ignorant; they could not afford for their works to be idle in order that they might pose as pioneers of taste.

The earliest landscape painting on English porcelain is found on Chelsea of the raised anchor period. This is dainty work, immature and tentative in style, and yet possessing the merit of originality.[1] A little later we recognize the hand of the 'Fable Painter', whose landscapes were painted either in polychrome[2] or in green, purple, or crimson monochrome in the style of the German factories – the 'purple landskips' of the Catalogues[3] belong to this class of work [78].[4] This detailed, carefully painted work is in a class by itself, and worlds apart from the heavier, more laborious style of the closing years of the factory, when such as Zachariah Boreman began to experiment with the styles which were taken to Derby.[5] The slighter work is at least equally decorative, but it is at the same time so much more fitting to the delicate fritt body, and the same may be said of the rare gold anchor painting in black and green referred to in a previous chapter, and of the strange landscapes in green, in the Meissen style of Lindener, which were listed by the auctioneer Burnsall in the 1776 sale, 'a fine old green landscape Chelsea quart bowl', and a 'Chelsea round tureen and cover painted in green landscape'. The early Chelsea painting had no counterpart at Bow, and not until 1760–65 was landscape painting attempted to any extent. This comparatively late period was not remarkable for excellence of decoration of any sort, either as regards style or technique, but the Bow lake scenes were handled sensitively, they are well spaced, and have a refreshing, clean look about them,[6] although the palette was restricted to red-brown, green, and purple. At Longton Hall the very rare attempts at landscape work are painstakingly true to life, full of detail, and subdued in colour,[7] as are also the equally uncommon Lowestoft examples. Mr Kiddell has been able to identify one of the artists,[8] a Richard Powles, whose signed pieces show him to have been a skilled painter of coastal scenes and shipping, meticulous as to detail, and expert at the rendering of vigorous cloud effects. Mr Kiddell has suggested that the same hand may have been responsible for the Meissen-like 'classic ruins' in puce enamel which are rarely found on Lowestoft wares.

There is a marked similarity between the Worcester landscapes of the 1760s and those of Chelsea, since the Meissen style was the inspiration of both factories. Simple little landscapes were painted,[9] and small, tidy vignettes of hunting scenes or combats,[10] though occasionally larger scenes were spread out over more important pieces.[11] As usual, the early Worcester painters must perforce remain anonymous, though it is

[1]Herbert Allen Collection, pl 23, nos 84 and 85; Schreiber Collection, no 155.
[2]Old English Porcelain, Honey, pl 5b. [3]Ibid, pls 6a, 8a and b, 10b; Herbert Allen Collection, pl 23, no 84.
[4]Figures within brackets refer to plates at the back of this book. [5]V & A. Museum, nos 172 and 172A.
[6]Old English Porcelain, Honey, pl 34; Schreiber Collection, no 104; V. & A. Museum, 3272–1853.
[7]Schreiber Collection, pl 53, no 443.
[8]English Ceramic Circle, Transactions, no 7, vol 2, 1939, pls XXXVII–XXXIX.
[9]Old English Porcelain, Honey, pl 59a. [10]Worcester Porcelain, Hobson, pl LVII, nos 1 and 2.
[11]Worcester Porcelain, Barrett, pls 13, 14 and 46.

recorded that in the late 1760s a painter named Fogo specialized in landscapes. Nightingale speaks of a 'pair of very finely painted plates in landscapes, and signed C. C. Fogo, with the date 1768', but all trace of them is lost, and Binns makes no mention of a signature in his description of a pair from the Nightingale Collection, which might otherwise answer to the description.[1] Later, about 1770, more detailed painting was accompanied by the fine, deep blue Worcester ground colour, or else was bordered with turquoise husk pattern or shagreen, and surrounded by birds, insects, and fruit.[2] To this period belong the first attempts at landscape painting in monochrome,[3] usually sepia, when the delicate, subdued scenery in this style was used as a background to the several varieties of 'exotic birds'.[4] The last phase, during the decade preceding Wall's death, produced landscapes lacking the delicacy of the earlier ones, with emphatic colours and bright, hard clouds,[5] though occasionally one may see an exceptional piece in which good composition and drawing, and clear harmonizing colours combine to rival anything which had gone before.[6]

Just as Derby specialized in local views and nearby country mansions, so did the three later Worcester factories, but because certain views near the city had more than a local interest we find that such buildings as Worcester Cathedral [90] and Malvern Priory were treated in many different ways, and form the centres of interest of many compositions. These subjects, and many others, are usually bordered by or reserved upon the fine ground colours in which all three factories excelled, notably claret, maroon, apple-green, and blue, but it is not possible in most cases to name the artists. It is however certain that there are few styles of landscape painting which cannot be found on both Flights and Chamberlains wares, though the Grainger factory had little part in the working of its more established neighbours. The names of the artists who are known to have done this branch of decoration at one or both of the factories are as follows – John Smith, E. Doe, Silk, Robert Brewer, Moses Webster, and C. Hayton, and, of course, landscapes are often an intrinsic part of the specialized figure painting of James Pennington, Thomas Baxter, and Humphrey Chamberlain. We are able to identify much of their work, and we cannot do better than to begin with Chamberlain. One would not, I think, call him an artist in the full sense of the word, for though his work has a minuteness which gave reason for his claim to invisible brush-strokes it is a laborious minuteness, and he had little knowledge of how to gain effect by economy of line and shade, particularly in his figure subjects. On the other

[1] *Worcester Porcelain*, p 88.
[2] *Ibid*, Hobson, pl LXXIII; Frank Lloyd Collection, pl 41, no 203; Schreiber Collection, pl 58, no 598; Herbert Allen Collection, pl 55, no 274. [3] *Worcester Porcelain*, Hobson, pl XCIX, no 1.
[4] Frank Lloyd Collection, pl 42, nos 207 and 207a, pl 51, no 253.
[5] *Ibid*, pl 41, no 203; [6] *Old English Porcelain*, Honey, pl 77c.

hand, some lovely landscapes by his hand are seen as the backgrounds to his copies of the engravings in 'Rural Sports' (by J. Scott after W. B. Daniell),[1] which go far to justify his claim to have been the foremost of the Worcester landscape painters [89]. Thomas Baxter was at Worcester from 1814 to 1816, and again, after a break at Swansea, from 1819 until his death in 1821, and he is, of course, best known for his painting of scenes from Shakespeare and Scott.[2] He was nevertheless extremely versatile, and his rather misty, brooding backgrounds to such scenes are minutely and carefully executed. His best work in this regard is to be seen on a service decorated with dancers in landscape setting, made in 1815 for the Nabob of Oude. James Pennington came to Flights from Etruria in 1792, and he stayed there for over fifty years, during which time he specialized in such symbolical subjects as his well-known emblematical figures of Truth, Justice, Fortitude, Conjugal Peace, and Hope, the last mentioned with backgrounds of well-painted stormy sea and lowering clouds [117].[3] Much of his work was painted in sepia monochrome,[4] but he also painted rustic figures against backgrounds outstanding for their freshness and brightness of pure colour.

Of the others, who were purely landscape painters, the work of E. Doe is easily recognizable for its clear resemblance to the printed landscapes upon Pratt earthenware.[5] His rather thick 'oil painting' style features hazy distances, often with a purplish effect as of distant rain, with white sheep in the foreground and sunlight shining upon whitewashed walls. Robert Brewer painted upon Flights porcelain and on Chamberlains, and his style is typified by a series of Irish views on a service made at the latter factory in his well-known brownish-greens, browns, and madders, with 'wiped-out', heavy cumulus clouds, grey tinted, and water shaded in horizontal grey dashes [88]. There were several painters who specialized in 'architectural' drawing, one of whom was particularly fond of sunlit evening scenes with long, grey shadows, dark blue sky, and deep pink clouds shading to yellow on the horizon; his buildings are accurately drawn, as if with a ruler, and washed in with strong, brick-red tones [90]. In scenery on a wider scale, a Chamberlain artist was responsible for windy, 'mackerel' skies, an amazing variety of greens, minutely drawn foliage, touches of red or purple (usually in the form of foxgloves), and lavish use of white in figures in the foreground. Another worked in Banford's Derby style on small cabinet pieces, with brown and green washed over a neutral foundation, and pale skies with pink and grey washed into the blue. Among several artists who worked in monochrome was he who drew carelessly, relying upon his good composition for his effect, with boldly drawn

1 *Worcester Porcelain*, Hobson, pl cvi, fig 5; Herbert Allen Collection, pl 65, no 372.
2 *Worcester Porcelain*, Hobson, pl cv, fig 1. 3 *Ibid*, pl cv, fig 2. 4 Catalogue of the Works Museum, no 1183.
5 *19th Century English Pottery and Porcelain*, Bemrose, pl 64A.

figures and cattle in the foreground. Abbeys and castles were peculiar to a Flight decorator, minutely drawn, with yellow foreground shaded with sepia, grey distant hills, greyish-blue clouds in a blue sky, reddish rocks, and brown-green foliage. A rather depressing Flights style is usually found in conjunction with an apple-green border, the colours are basically grey-tinted with the exception of a patch of stone-work or foliage lit by the sun, and the sky is coldly blue [87]. The views painted by another are contrastingly gay, in sunny greens, framed by dark, grey-green trees and bushes in the foreground.

Comparatively little landscape work was done at Graingers, though an early artist (about 1830) painted views of Worcester Bridge and the Cathedral with fine detail in brilliant reds and browns, with pink-centred 'wiped-out' clouds in a pale blue sky, and with figures and shadows in dark grey. Important pieces of the later years, up to about 1850, were occasionally decorated by an artist who in his favourite river scenes used an extensive palette of rather weak but bright enamels, and who specialized in gaily clothed figures, well-drawn boats, and most carefully painted reflections. The total effect is often that of a water-colour.

Speaking by and large, the painting at Worcester took the shape of instances of versatility on the part of all-round decorators, but at Derby it was a branch of decoration carried out by specialists. It is not quite clear why this should have been so, though the presence of so many important mansions nearby, and the lovely scenery of the Derwent region, may have influenced Duesbury's policy. It is certain, at any rate, that not ornamental pieces only, but also complete services were ordered by the local gentry to be painted with views of their estates. As in the case of other classes of Derby decoration those responsible for the finer landscapes are known by name and their work can usually be identified. The earliest was almost certainly Zachariah Boreman, who we remember as a Chelsea workman and probably as the chief landscape painter there. He came to Derby in 1783 and returned to London to work for Simms in 1794, and during that time he is known to have painted over four thousand landscapes in that careful style which, as head over the painters, he was obliged to maintain.[1] He painted from nature, and his subjects commonly include a vista of winding river, with minute but suggestive figures in the foreground. His technique was that of the water-colourist, in that he washed in his picture with a neutral tint, with his colours laid over in transparent washes before the first firing. Then, with a finer brush (or 'tracing pencil') he hatched and stippled and applied the last finer details. His colours are soft and subdued, with an extensive use of greys and greens

[1]*Old Derby Porcelain*, Hurlbutt, pls 27 and 28; *Old English Porcelain*, Honey, pl 44c; Herbert Allen Collection, pl 29, no 161; Schreiber Collection, pl 48, no 413; *Crown Derby Porcelain*, Gilhespy, fig 41.

against which are contrasted the gayer-coloured figures in red and orange. His skies are ochre, with neutral tinted clouds, the edges wiped out with the wooden end of the brush.

James Banford worked at Derby from 1789 to 1795, so that he was contemporary with Boreman. He had been apprenticed at Bristol as a flower painter, and before making his way to Derby it is probable that he worked for some time in London, where Major Tapp has suggested that he may have painted on Chelsea-Derby wares. At Derby he specialized in the decoration of the small cabinet pieces in which the factory excelled, not only with landscapes but also with figures and flowers, and no less than sixteen patterns were assigned to him, according to the Cup and Saucer Pattern Book. He worked in a style so similar to that of Boreman that it is difficult to distinguish between their work. Like his rival he favoured little figures in the foreground, but they are seldom so brightly coloured. The stippling of his trees is often vertical, and he made use of effective contrasts of bright yellow and green, blue, and mauve. His foliage is sometimes of an olive-green colour, and he had a liking for sheep and for slanting bands of light across his trees. One is often tempted to think that Banford was the better artist – that he himself was of that opinion is evident from his correspondence with Duesbury, for in one letter he wrote that 'when there is anything minute or requires neatness, my optic nerves are to be strained for 18/– per week less (than Boreman).'

When Boreman went to London his place was filled until 1800 by Thomas Hill, usually known as 'Jockey Hill' because of his fondness for horses. Duesbury's aim was to continue what had become a popular style, and that of the new-comer was very like that of his predecessor, with the same first application of neutral colour, even the same contrasting figures in the foreground.[1] There are differences, however, for Hill's colours are brighter, with yellows and greens instead of greys and greens, especially for fields, with the stippling more finely applied, and the figures rustic rather than fashionable, and often accompanied by dogs. Moreover, his landscapes were not always taken from nature, for many of his subjects are recognizable in Middiman's *Select Views of Great Britain*, published in 1784.

The outstanding Derby landscape painters of the turn of the century were the Brewer brothers, Robert and John, but although the work of one or other is to be seen in many collections[2] their styles are so similar that it is difficult to distinguish between them, even though Robert's work at Worcester before he went to Derby in

[1]*Old Derby Porcelain*, Hurlbutt, pls 29–32; *Crown Derby Porcelain*, Gilhespy, fig 53.
[2]*Old Derby Porcelain*, Hurlbutt, pls 33, 34 and 56; Herbert Allen Collection, pl 34, no 136; *Crown Derby Porcelain*, Gilhespy, figs 65–67.

1797 can be identified, as can some of his 'camp scenes' which are listed in the Pattern Books. For his part John is known to have painted views of shipping in water-colour style.[1] Both departed from the Boreman technique, for they painted their subjects directly in the positive colours, which after firing were strengthened where necessary, and the details added. Opaque chrome-green replaced the translucent copper-green of Boreman, Hill, and Banford, and both used a great variety of warm browns, madders, and reds. Skies were painted in light blue, heavy cumulus clouds were swept out, leaving the edges hard, and were then shaded in with neutral tints and ochre. Robert's hand is often betrayed by his habit of depicting foliage in small clusters like the fingers and thumb of a hand, and both wiped out their highlights, just as Billingsley did with his roses, leaving just a hint of colour behind.

The work of the succeeding painters either overlaps into the Bloor period or else falls entirely within its compass. Haslem writes of the truth, and suitability for engravings, of the work of George Robertson (1796–1820), and this artist's style is usually in fact recognizable by reason of his partiality for pleasing autumn tints, though his colours are apt to be thick and his stippling coarse.[2] Jesse Mountford was remarkable for his minute stippling and for his characteristic clarity in the drawing of his rocks and buildings, so that Gilhespy speaks of his work as possessing a 'drop curtain' effect.[3] Cuthbert Lawton painted with 'an agreeable freshness and a look of nature', to quote Haslem again, and there is a tradition that he was a painter of hunting scenes.[4] William Cordon liked panoramic views, and McLacklan is noted for his use of dark monochrome which gives an 'Indian Ink' appearance to his work.[5]

Of the later painters who stayed at Derby until the close, one only is outstanding, Daniel Lucas, who began work in the early 1830s and who had been trained at Longport. His work is much superior to that of his anonymous contemporaries, for his treatment of foliage on rather trembly branches shows considerable attention to detail, though in common with them he used the oil-painter's technique, with strong, thick, paint-like enamels, so that the character of the porcelain beneath is often quite lost.[6]

There is little to choose between the styles of landscape painting at Derby and Pinxton, since most of the Pinxton artists were Derby men, among them James Hadfield and Edward Rowland. Billingsley painted landscapes as well as flowers,[7] when he painted at all, and some carelessly painted scenery in the style of Boreman, with

[1]*Old English Porcelain*, Honey, pl 44*b*.
[2]Herbert Allen Collection, pl 39, no 156, and no 185; *Crown Derby Porcelain*, Gilhespy, figs 59 and 60.
[3]Herbert Allen Collection, pl 38, no 143; *Crown Derby Porcelain*, Gilhespy, fig 72.
[4]*Crown Derby Porcelain*, Gilhespy, fig 73. [5]*Ibid*, fig 74.
[6]Herbert Allen Collection, pl 40, no 183; pl 36, no 142. [7]*Nantgarw Porcelain*, John, pl 37*c*.

lavish use of pale red and yellowish brown was the work of John Cutts, who painted also at Etruria upon the very little porcelain made there. Haslem refers to pieces painted with circular views of Derbyshire, and a panoramic view was sometimes used to stretch entirely around a suitably shaped piece. [1]

Landscapes at Coalport were not popular before about 1860, though even during the Caughley years one may see an occasional exception. Thus, the same muddy sepia enamel used for flowers was sometimes used for monochrome painting of landscapes, while in polychrome comparatively poorly drawn subjects were painted in a weak palette, with watery green distances, dingy brown foregrounds, and pink clouds. [2] After Rose's move to Coalport it was the usual practice for the more elaborate decoration to be done elsewhere, notably at Baxter's Clerkenwell studios, until that prolific artist moved to Flights in 1814. It is suspected, without proof other than that afforded by style, that Fidelle Duvivier may have included Coalport wares among those which he decorated while working independently at New Hall, about 1790.

After 1815, and until about 1840, landscapes similar to those of Derby were painted inside the factory, for the same reason as that which dictated Pinxton style. Bloor discharged Jesse Mountford about 1821, and shortly afterwards his name appeared in the Coalport pattern books, together with signed examples of his work, in watercolour. Another workman with a Derby background was Thomas Steele, son of the Derby fruit painter, who is commended by Haslem as 'showing promise' as a landscape painter and who, at Coalport, specialized in Scottish scenery. Every factory inevitably developed its own particular styles, and in this regard we see at Coalport a leaning towards misty distances [3] in the 'open air' style we have already mentioned, and a desire to take advantage of wealthy patronage which in this case took the form of pictures of important places such as the Royal palaces which were painted on rococo vases. Landscapes often include figures in the styles of Watteau or Lancret. [4]

It is a natural move from Coalport to the Welsh potteries. The decoration on both is indeed very similar, for at Nantgarw very little painting was done, the ware being sent to London for that purpose, [5] and the only name which can be linked up with factory landscape work is that of William Weston Young, who was a good amateur water-colourist and who published in 1835 his *Guide to the beauties etc of Glyn Neath*. There are pieces in existence which would seem to bear sufficiently strong resemblance to its illustrations as to make it probable that they were painted by the same hand. [6]

So great was the emphasis on flower painting at Swansea that landscapes were seldom attempted. Young's hand is occasionally seen, [7] and Billingsley painted a few

[1]Herbert Allen Collection, pl 42, no 202. [2]Barrett, fig 61. [3]*Idem*, fig 93. [4]*Idem*, fig 99.
[5]Herbert Allen Collection, pl 72, no 418. [6]*Nantgarw Porcelain*, John, pl 35b. [7]*Ibid*, pl 35a.

charming subjects in simple green enamels or in sepia, [1] while his 'garden scenery' on a service made for Mr Dillwyn is clear proof that his genius was not confined to ordinary flower painting. We meet Baxter again [91], for in 1818 he published some views of the neighbourhood, and on porcelain he is known to have painted views of noblemen's houses. [2] George Beddow is little more than a name, but he is reputed to have painted well into the Bevington era, in crude colours or in monochrome.

Landscape painting was alien to the true taste of Plymouth and Bristol, and when seen at all it is usually incidental to other styles of decoration. Prideaux says of 'Mons. Soqui' [3] that he was 'an excellent painter and enameller', and certainly his landscapes which accompany his 'exotic birds', but which are rarely found alone, fully justify that assessment. [4] Henry Bone is reputed to have painted at Bristol for a short time, but there can be little certainty in the attribution of specific examples of landscape painting to him, although he may have been responsible for a few carefully drawn studies in crimson monochrome, [5] and for some insignificant but dainty little polychrome sketches.

In the Potteries, landscape painting was developed during the middle of the 19th century, when the demand for colour resulted in magnificent but laboured decoration of every conceivable sort. Derby workmen were responsible for a great deal of it, for their new employers were not always content to allow them to retain their comparatively reticent styles. At Mintons monochrome painting was of excellent quality, and John Cutts painted scenery at Etruria which is clean-looking and fresh, though characteristically careless [86]. By 1800 porcelain making at Spodes was in full swing, and landscapes [6] were applied to wares made in classical style, ornate and richly gilt, and to plaques in the Derby style. Josiah II was ever catholic in his search for models, and the landscapes of the period are all too often merely imaginative 'views', lacking in real character, and plainly inspired by second-rate water-colourists. Nevertheless, there are outstanding exceptions, though even in the most accomplished work it is always obvious that inspiration derived from the paintings of masters in another field of art, and that painting was hardly ever original.

Some of the best of all mid 19th century landscape painting was done at a factory which is almost completely ignored by most writers, the Cauldon pottery established by Job Ridgway at the end of the previous century. It was the son, John, who took over in 1814 and who developed good decoration on the porcelain which he evolved – good, that is, in the sense that it is of the highest quality, although it made no claim

---

[1] *Swansea and Nantgarw Potteries*, Meager, pl VIII, no 32. [2] *Ibid*, pl XIII, no 344.
[3] Schreiber Collection, pl 85, no 740. [4] V. & A. Museum, no C109–1919.
[5] *Old English Porcelain*, Honey, pl 92c. [6] *Ibid*, opp p 170.

to be other than 'oil painting on porcelain'. A typical example of this sort of work is a remarkable plaque bearing a view of Windsor Castle, in which the picture is actually 'framed' by a most intricate rococo moulding in porcelain. We may or may not admire such a masterpiece of technical and decorative skill, which is nevertheless chosen as being typical of the modern tendency in landscape painting. One thing only is certain, that a well-painted landscape on porcelain can be appreciated apart from the quality of the porcelain beneath it, and enjoyment of any sort of art can never be a bad thing.

CHAPTER NINE

Bird Painting

Broadly spoken there are three types of bird painting on porcelain, apart from those of purely Oriental form – the exotic, the naturalistic, and the transitional, by which we mean birds of reasonably natural shape but with unnaturally gay colouring. The art of painting birds is not a difficult one, for they lend themselves to detailed though uninspired copying, and lack of drawing skill may be compensated for in some measure by the use of brilliant colour. There has been no period when ordinary English birds of the more colourful varieties have not been painted on English porcelain – the stuffed bird is even now a familiar model in many a decorating department – but there is considerable difference between groups of birds posed naturally in their proper surroundings and single specimens, however lovely, perched stiffly in the centre of a plate. The 'exotic bird' is a gorgeous creature of the imagination, happy and joyful, fantastic, impossible, but as perfect an ornament on porcelain as has ever been conceived. The original inspiration was the Golden Pheasant, perhaps crossed with the phoenix, developed into the *'fantasievögel'* of Meissen, and perfected at Sèvres by such painters as Evans and Aloncle before Worcester claimed it in the 1770s. The natural camouflage of many a humble English or foreign bird was transformed by the substitution of bright enamels and gold into the creatures of the third class, creatures which could not long survive in their new plumage save on a piece of porcelain, but which there have undoubted decorative value.

When the Bow painters attempted a change from the Kakiemon birds, they preferred this transitional style of painting, and the humble brown or red quail or partridge took upon himself a quite alien splendour. In another way, too, the artist was able to indulge his craving for colour by choosing real birds which were naturally colourful and which needed but little elaboration, birds such as the cockatoo or the pheasant.[1] Very rarely did they copy the exotic type, sometimes from Chelsea[2] and sometimes, later, from Worcester,[3] though it must never be forgotten that the hand of the outside decorator was always at work.

Leaving on one side for a moment the enthusiastic specialization at Worcester and

[1] *Bow Porcelain*, Hurlbutt, pl 19a. [2] Schreiber Collection, no 105. [3] *Ibid*, no 107.

Chelsea, we find occasional bird painting at all the early factories. At Longton Hall, for instance, both naturalistic and exotic ones were painted in landscape settings as alternatives to flowers in the spaces reluctantly left for them on the typical rococo vases, bristling with applied flowers, or placed in the centre of plates, with moulded borders, in typical Worcester style. More rarely we see very attractive little bird studies of Oriental origin. Caughley copies of the Worcester exotic birds are comparatively poor,[1] as is most of the early Salopian decoration, because of the use of inferior colours allied to a lack of spontaneity, and the early days at Derby contribute little save some rather clumsily drawn birds of the transitional variety which were possibly the work of the 'moth painter'.

The Sèvres influence which was always so pronounced at Chelsea was responsible for the abundant bird painting found on its wares, at least as regards that of the more flamboyant exotic variety. At the same time, even in those early days certain artists were extremely successful with their naturalistic birds [93],[2] which were daintily painted though essentially simple and natural in conception,[3] and far superior to the rather wooden creatures attempted at Worcester at about the same time. It is of course possible that this style of work, too, may have had its inspiration in the sort of painting as practised at the French factory by such painters as Tandart. The Meissen custom of painting in crimson monochrome was adapted for birds as well as for landscapes,[4] and the 'Fable painter' clearly did his share in this regard.[5] So far as exotic birds are concerned we should naturally expect a marked similarity between those of Chelsea and Worcester; before the closing of the former it was a matter of successful imitation, and afterwards many of the London artists continued their work at the latter factory.[6] As at Bow, it seems clear that much of the finer decoration in this as in other styles was done outside the factory, such as the well-known 'dishevelled' or 'agitated' birds of the early years, and the naturalistic ones of the later, painted after Hondekoeter on the important vases in Sèvres style, quite possibly by John Donaldson. We should not omit mention, before passing on to the Worcester developments, of the rather ornate but beautifully painted peacocks and peahens, in tooled gold on a blue ground, of the gold anchor period (a style copied successfully at Mintons and Coalport many years later), or the contemporary stylized pheasants in green, with their elaborate gilding and their tendency towards the exotic.

The long-tailed birds and quail-like creatures of the Redcliff Backs factory, beautiful

---

[1]Barrett, fig 64. [2]Figures within brackets refer to plates at the back of this book.
[3]*Old English Porcelain*, Honey, pls 18*a* and 20*a*; Herbert Allen Collection, pl 21, nos 93 and 94; Schreiber Collection, pl 28, no 215. [4]British Museum, Barwell Bequest. [5]Herbert Allen Collection, no 63.
[6]*Old English Porcelain*, Honey, pl 20*b*.

as they are, gave little promise of the splendour to come when the Worcester decorators should ally the exotic birds to their scale patterns, perfected ground colours, and impeccable honey gilding, thus exemplifying their usual good taste, and evolving a style which is the most typical of all these practised at the factory. It would be a mistake to imagine that all the exotic birds are necessarily of the finest quality, for they were not only used on important specimens but also on entire services, when it is common to find that the pieces bear rather stiff repetitions of a fixed model which was presumably copied from a book of engraved designs.

Of the finer work there are numerous styles, and we may mention first that of the outside decorator, probably from Giles's studio, who painted not only Worcester but also Bow, Chelsea, Longton Hall, Derby, and Bristol wares.[1] His birds have been called 'dishevelled' or 'agitated' [92], and they are moreover unkempt, though full of life and free from the gaudiness which tends to mar some of the other styles. We know that Sprimont founded a school of painters at Chelsea, that the *Public Advertiser* announced in 1768 that the Worcester proprietors had engaged 'the best painters from Chelsea', and that in May 1769 an eight day sale was held in London of pieces bearing all sorts of decoration, including birds, 'curiously painted'. It is therefore certain that among the Londoners were several bird painters, including one who painted in bold, flowing strokes of a full brush,[2] and who can be fairly identified with the fruit painter whose trademark was the fig with calyx and the sliced fruit. The characteristic style of his painting leads us to recognize his birds by their thin, spindly legs, and their small wings with ruffled feathers.

The sleek, plump birds [94], brilliant and flaunting, with goitred necks and 'dowager' appearance,[3] were probably the work of the same 'Mons. Soqui' who worked at Bristol, and whose thick stippling and pale-tinted distant landscape backgrounds with red-brown foregrounds and tree-trunks are in the same style as that of the noted Sèvres artist, Evans. The identity of the painter of the bird with the staring, circular eyes is unknown, though since his style (though not his brushwork) is found also on Liverpool and Longton Hall specimens it is at least possible that he and other artists had a common source of inspiration, presumably an engraving from which they copied. The bodies of these birds are formed of S-shaped curves, the plumage painted in dots, the wings small and closed, and the tails in-curving, while the foliage of the landscape setting was usually rendered in red.[4]

[1] *Worcester Porcelain*, Hobson, pls LXXXVII and LXXXVIII, fig 5.
[2] *Old English Porcelain*, Honey, pl 71a and c.
[3] *Ibid*, pl 73a; *Worcester Porcelain*, Hobson, pls LXXXVI, fig 2 and XCIV.
[4] *Old English Porcelain*, pl 71a; Frank Lloyd Collection, pl 50, no 252; *Worcester Porcelain*, Hobson, pls XC and XCI; Schreiber Collection, nos 552 and 554.

The manner of another painter, who like Soqui seems to have worked at Bristol for some time, is characterized by birds with long bodies and necks, [1] and another favoured the painting of plumage in the peculiar Worcester dry lapis-lazuli blue, with faint and distant settings. [2] The usual landscape backgrounds do indeed provide valuable aid to the classification of the various styles, for a certain blunt spikiness is invariably accompanied by smudgy brushwork and an absence of 'dotted' plumage, [3] and a painter who otherwise worked in the Soqui style preferred strong, clear landscape in which the trees are like cumulus cloud. [4]

We have already said that the Worcester naturalistic birds are inclined to woodenness, even though they are peaceful-looking and invariably well painted. [5] At the same time there are notable exceptions, as, for instance, the rare and beautiful work of the 'Fable painter' in this style, as exemplified by the well-known subject of an owl on a branch, mobbed by other birds, [6] before a landscape background of poplars. Transitional birds from the factory are pleasing in shape though often impossibly exotic in colour, and the designs in which they occur are always well spaced and well balanced. [7]

At this juncture the kinship between the exotic birds of Worcester and those of Plymouth and Bristol is sufficient excuse to warrant an excursion into the alien realms of 'hard paste'. Little is known about Soqui, except that he came from Sèvres, and worked under both Cookworthy and Champion. His style is unmistakable, on whatever porcelain his work is seen. [8] The hand of the Giles artist is often recognizable, [9] and also that of he who painted the Worcester birds with the stretched necks. [10] Mackenna has suggested that this unknown copier was an outside decorator working in Bristol or London, and this is indeed very probable. Certainly his birds cannot be confused with those of the Giles man, in that they lack the typical hunched appearance, the outspread, brilliant plumage, and the predominantly green backgrounds. The style of a fourth artist is very like that of Soqui, but the colours and drawing alike are more delicate (though giving a flatter effect), and there is an absence of elaborate background. Naturalistic birds are commonly in the style of Derby and Swansea, [11] and were reserved for smaller pieces such as mugs. Although posed in natural surround-

[1] *Worcester Porcelain*, Hobson, pl XCII. [2] *Ibid*, pl LXX.
[3] *Old English Porcelain*, Honey, pl 72a; *Schreiber Collection*, pl 57, no 550; *Frank Lloyd Collection*, pl 55, no 265. [4] *Old English Porcelain*, Honey, pl 72b.
[5] *Worcester Porcelain*, Hobson, pl LXXXVIII, figs 1 and 4; *Frank Lloyd Collection*, pl 5, no 110a, pl 20, no 112. [6] *Schreiber Collection*, pl 68, no 474. [7] *Worcester Porcelain*, Hobson, pl XCIII.
[8] *Bristol Porcelain*, Hurlbutt, pls 3, 21a and 49b; *Champion's Bristol Porcelain*, Mackenna, fig 1.
[9] *Champion's Bristol Porcelain*, Mackenna, fig 3; *Schreiber Collection*, pl 85, no 740; *Bristol Porcelain*, Hurlbutt, pl 39a. [10] *Cookworthy's Plymouth and Bristol Porcelain*, Mackenna, fig 56.
[11] *Champion's Bristol Porcelain*, Mackenna, fig 61.

ings they are stiff and often so badly drawn that it is difficult to identify them with any living creature.

While at Worcester bird painting was gradually being forsaken (apart from some later work at Flights, in Soqui style, by a painter named Davis), at Derby a great deal was being done, not as a speciality but in answer to the demand for services painted with naturalistic birds. One may suspect, too, that there was somewhat of a belated effort to take advantage of the Worcester change of fashion. At an earlier date the exotic birds had been neglected, if we except a few solitary ones in little detached landscapes painted in the late 1750s by the 'moth painter',[1] and both Boreman and John Brewer were later called upon to paint exotic birds in the Chelsea style. Boreman used his usual neutral tints and subdued positives worked over and stippled, with copper-green foliage and honey gold,[2] while Brewer applied his thicker pigments direct, using opaque chrome-green and burnished gold. Richard Dodson painted fine transitional and naturalistic birds and although his colours are apt to be unnaturally bright and gay his birds are never lifeless because he placed them in their natural surroundings in well-spaced groups.[3] George Complin painted the smaller English birds as incidental accompaniments to his fruit and landscapes, and William Dexter, working during the period 1830-50, either by himself or with one or other of the Hancocks (a well-known family of Derby workmen), painted birds in the Sèvres style so effectively that it is probable that the intention was to deceive.[4] Among other styles of bird painting must be mentioned some rather gloomy work in gold upon a black ground, after Bewick engravings, which is found on a mourning service made about 1812.

Bird painting at Coalport, the other member of the 'Big Three' of the 1800-50 period, was not abundant, and was with few exceptions confined to imitations of the Worcester exotic type. John Randall did them extremely well, as did his uncle, Thomas Martin Randall, at Madeley,[5] after he had given up his decorating studio in London [97]. Both painted in the Sèvres style, John in such a manner as to become as famous for his birds as Billingsley was for his roses, and Thomas to such purpose that his Madeley wares have often passed, and doubtless will still pass, for the true *pâte tendre*. Working at the same time as Randall was Mottershead, whose name appears many times in the pattern books, and whose long-legged birds are painted in a bright blue, vivid yellow, brick-red, and puce, with long, graceful necks, and perched on tree stumps from which spring the spidery branches which are the only background.[6]

[1]*Crown Derby Porcelain*, Gilhespy, figs 3 and 4. [2]*Old Derby Porcelain*, Hurlbutt, pl 45.
[3]*Ibid*, pls 48 and 49; *Crown Derby Porcelain*, Gilhespy, figs 76 and 77.
[4] *Ibid*, Gilhespy, figs 88-90. [5]Barrett, fig 160. [6] *Idem*, fig 97.

In Wales, as we have gathered, most of the Nantgarw painting was foreign to the factory. Some pieces bear small birds, carefully and delicately painted, accompanied by a raised *bleu-du-roi* border, [1] and others seem to have been done by Randall before the Madeley days, in a style which features large birds together with several smaller ones, usually three in number. Finest of all are the transitional birds of the Mackintosh Service [99], in which each piece is brilliantly painted with a single large bird chosen for its colour, in multi-hued tones of an extensive palette in which red, orange, blue, and black predominate. [2] Other recorded names are those of Thomas Pardoe [3] and John Latham (before he left to go to Worcester and Coalport), but factory work is extremely rare. At Swansea, Matthew Colclough [4] and William Weston Young are reputed to have painted natural birds, and Thomas Baxter also [119], for he was at home with every sort of painting, but as at Nantgarw the elaborate work was sent out to be done elsewhere, [5] and the factory artists confined their attentions to comparatively simple repetitive work. [6]

The wide scope offered by bird life to porcelain painters seems unaccountably to have been largely ignored by the Staffordshire men, possibly because the industrialists who supported them demanded either the gay and obviously expensive Japans or the flowers and landscapes which they could better understand. Doubtless in their eyes the exotic bird was downright un-English and unpractical, and the naturalistic one too feminine. Theirs was the porcelain of the dining-room rather than that of the boudoir. Whatever the reason, in the Potteries birds were out of favour on porcelain, though naturally enough the pattern books of most factories included a few patterns which featured them. Mintons, for example, had a painter who painted large tom-tits and finches feather by feather on large vases, and Spodes could on occasion excel in this as in every other sort of decoration. One is tempted to wonder why a factory so fecund in design did not at least attempt to revive the Worcester exotic bird and scale pattern, for it was certainly powerful enough to set a fashion. A reason has been suggested, and certainly the existing patterns were popular enough to make fresh departures unnecessary. The nearest approach was in fact a style of decoration allied to that of the Nantgarw Mackintosh Service, the painting of 'natural' exotic birds rather than the fantastic ones, which is seen at its best on the lovely 'Whitebait Service' [7] numbered 2102 in the Pattern Book. The birds are real birds, but with their brilliant colours slightly exaggerated, a different one to each piece, bordered by a

[1]*Nantgarw Porcelain*, John, coloured illustration, no 15a. [2]*Ibid*, coloured illustration, no 24.
[3]*Ibid*, pls 54a and b, 55a, 56a, b, c, and d.
[4]Schreiber Collection, pl 91, no 801; V. & A. Museum, no 3490–1901.
[5]Herbert Allen Collection, pl 73, no 419. [6]*Swansea and Nantgarw Potteries*, Meager, pl XII, no 66.
[7]*Spode and his Successors*, Hayden, opp p 164.

warm buff band on which feathers are delicately painted. Much the same style was used on more important pieces, such as ornate vases [1] gilded with foliate designs at base and neck, and with the painting framed with arabesque ornament. A style of decoration which Josiah Spode II made virtually his own, made use of matt gold against coloured grounds, notably maroon or claret, giving an entirely different effect from that which is seen, for example, on the Chelsea mazarine and gold cabinet pieces. The delicate gilding was probably done by Daniell. Much bird painting in earlier styles which is found on Spode porcelain is the result of the practice of making replacements for older damaged services [101]. Every factory of importance has always been asked at various times to undertake this sort of work, and Spodes copied the wares of Chelsea, Derby, Worcester, and even Sèvres. However excellent it may be the painting on such pieces is of little interest from the collector's point of view.

Mention has already been made of the fact that most bird painting on porcelain was not intended to be naturalistic. It will have been gathered, furthermore, that when it was so the effect is inclined to be stiff and stereotyped. The effectiveness of the 'exotic bird' as a decorative motif has never been in doubt; it is virtually a piece of design of which every sweeping curve is an intended part, and it is a capital vehicle for brilliant colours. A naturalistic bird, on the other hand, has no true beauty when it is dead, and even the skill of a Pardoe cannot give it vitality. For this reason most bird paintings on porcelain are more effective when the bird is part of a composition than when he is depicted, however skilfully, by himself.

[1] *Spode and his Successors, Hayden,* opp p 116.

CHAPTER TEN

Figure Painting

If we agree to except the figure painting in Oriental style which has already been discussed we are left with a class of decoration which offers less opportunity for study than any other, because comparatively little of it was done. Furthermore, though much porcelain of the 1770s does indeed carry superlative painting of this sort it is obvious that little was done inside the factories.

The figure painting of Chelsea was at first inspired by Meissen though the styles of Sèvres inevitably crept in at a later date. We find red anchor wares painted in cupids in light brick-red, a distinct Meissen style,[1] and from Sèvres came the fantastic '*chinoiseries*' of Pillement, painted in reserves on coloured grounds in the gold anchor years. These charming studies were painted in two styles, one of which is exemplified in the sumptuous Emily Thomson tea-service,[2] and the other which makes use of large figures very similar in style to those of Donaldson, but probably not by him, since his attention at that time is reputed to have been fully occupied in connexion with Worcester.[3] The same applies to figures painted in the style of Watteau and Teniers, while on the other hand those after Boucher[4] or Rubens may well be attributed to him, for they are found on the later imposing vases in Sèvres style which clearly demanded that degree of craftsmanship which he undoubtedly possessed. Figures in the Watteau style, copied from Chelsea, comprise practically the whole extent of the Bow work,[5] and they possess that simplicity and immature charm which is typical of so much of its polychrome decoration.

The early work at the two rival factories of Worcester and Derby followed on much the same lines, though from the latter came little apart from some very charming Watteau subjects relieved in panels on the fine *gros-bleu* ground.[6] The same style was adopted at Worcester, following after the still earlier hunting scenes and combats which were at first painted in vignettes and later used to extend over the surface of the ware. There were several painters in the Pillement manner, which is so fitted, in con-

[1]*Cheyne Book of Pottery and Porcelain*, pl 3, no 24; *Connoisseur*, September 1927, p 9.
[2]*Old English Porcelain*, Honey, pl 17a.
[3]*Cheyne Book of Pottery and Porcelain*, pl 24, no 83; *Chelsea Porcelain*, King, pl 54.
[4]Herbert Allen Collection, pls 15 and 16. [5]*Ibid*, pl 5, no 11; *Old English Porcelain*, Honey, pl 33.
[6]British Museum, nos IV–1 and 2.

junction with the scale patterns and ground colours, to the important vases to which it was applied.[1] On the whole, although figure subjects are common enough on Sèvres porcelain, this aspect of French decoration was never much imitated at Worcester, perhaps because there were no factory artists capable of copying it sufficiently well. Mention should nevertheless be made of an extremely early example of work which may be seen on the well-known 'cabbage-leaf' jugs in the Worcester Corporation Museum, painted with the city arms and the symbolical figures of Commerce and Justice,[2] and of certain reputed work of Wall himself[3] – reputed, and quite possibly authentic, for the hallmarks of the enthusiastic amateur are clearly visible in the drawing.

Donaldson and O'Neale were undoubtedly responsible for much of the finer Worcester figure painting, though whether they worked in the factory is still undecided. In his *Dictionary of Artists of the English School* Redgrave wrote that the former painted on Worcester[4] porcelain sent to London for that purpose, but Mr Honey has refuted this possibility on the plausible grounds that since the underglaze-blue grounds, subsidiary panels of flowers and birds, and final gilding were presumably applied in the factory, it would be unlikely that the factory authorities would risk the transport entailed. He points out also that whereas both artists used the peculiar dry lapis-lazuli blue in their Worcester figure subjects, this colour is not to be seen on London decorated wares. Certainly Donaldson lived in Worcester for some time, and he may have worked either in the factory or as a piece-worker in his own lodging. Jefferyes Hamett O'Neale, the painter of most of the fable subjects at Chelsea and Worcester, lived in the city from 1767 to 1769, but here again there is no evidence to prove that he was actually a factory employee. On the contrary, since so much of his work is signed[5] it is highly probable that he, too, worked at his own home, though we must not lose sight of the fact that an exception might well have been made in this regard for an artist of his pre-eminence. His large, boldly drawn figures, usually classical in subject, are prized for their perfection of brushwork, though their suitability as a porcelain decoration may be open to question.[6]

The delicately painted, graceful figures in classical style of the 1775–80 period[7] led to some specialized work of excellent quality which was done at both the later factories, but notably at Flights. Of James Pennington we have already spoken, for he was responsible for the Duke of Clarence service, on which the figure of Hope is

[1] *Worcester Porcelain, Hobson*, pls LXXIX, LXXXII, LXXXV, LXXXIX; Frank Lloyd Collection, nos 341–345, 354 and 355. [2] *Worcester Porcelain*, Hobson, pl C. [3] *Ibid*, pl V.
[4] *Ibid*, pls LXXIV, LXXVI–VIII and LXXX. [5] Frank Lloyd Collection, pl 73, nos 347 and 348.
[6] *Worcester Porcelain*, Hobson, pls LXXXIII and LXXXIV. [7] *Old English Porcelain*, Honey, pl 77*b*.

featured in numerous poses in a greenish sepia monochrome, boldly drawn, with detailed features, rounded limbs, and gracefully flowing draperies [117].[1] He was responsible for the sepia portraits of George III [116] and Queen Charlotte on the service in the Worcester Corporation Museum, for his monochrome emblematical figures,[2] and for some exquisite, fresh-coloured rural subjects,[3] usually female, painted in miniature style. He worked at Worcester for a period of about fifty years from 1792 onwards, and it is natural to suppose that most of the Flights figure painting (much of it on unmarked pieces) was done by him. As we have read in a previous chapter, Thomas Baxter painted at both factories, from 1814 to 1816, and again from 1819 to 1821. His rather brooding, melancholy style[4] is seen at its best on small cabinet pieces to which his short brush-strokes and decisive stippling are well suited.

The work of Humphrey Chamberlain junior is somewhat of an enigma, for if we may judge by the specimens he is reputed to have decorated, many of which are signed, he must have painted in two distinct styles. On the one hand there is the minutely painted, colourful 'Rural Sports' series, and an occasional outstanding piece of painting in classical style, in which the thick enamels are jewel-like in quality. On the other we find the delicate pastel shades and poorly drawn figures of the King of Hanover service [118]. No two styles could be more opposed, and at first glance one is tempted to discredit a common attribution. Only when they are carefully examined can a kinship be seen, for in both is the same painstaking technique, the same care to ensure that the individual brush-strokes are practically invisible. The probable explanation is that in the one instance Chamberlain was copying from well-drawn engravings, while in the other he was making original studies which would naturally betray his comparative lack of real drawing skill. This conclusion is corroborated by the existence of painting by him in which the stronger enamels were used, but in which the same immaturity of drawing is apparent, the same awkwardness in the limbs and in the pose of the heads. A small but interesting class of Chamberlain figure painting consists of slight, detached classical figures painted in sepia on a bright vermilion ground. Figure painting at Grainger's factory was usually reserved for important pieces, notably vases, on which we find panels containing mythical or classical scenes, carefully painted in an extensive palette of strong colours, and supported by subsidiary flower painting [122].

To return now to Derby, the outstanding painter of the 1770s was Richard Askew,

---

[1]Figures within brackets refer to plates at the back of this book.
[2]19th Century English Pottery and Porcelain, Bemrose, pl 55c.
[3]Herbert Allen Collection, pl 58, no 317.
[4]Ibid, pl 67, nos 376 and 377; 19th Century English Pottery and Porcelain, Bemrose, pl 55a.

whose earlier work as a piece-worker at Chelsea and later at Derby, in the Boucher style, was followed by specialization in the painting of Cupids.[1] The catalogue of 1771 refers to ware 'enamell'd in Cupids, after Busha', and Jewitt gives a long list of work done by him for Duesbury II at a much later date, in 1794–5, while he was living in Birmingham. Askew's cupids are so outstanding that they are worthy of description. The inspiration was entirely French, of course, but quite transformed into something essentially English; it has been said that he used his own children as his models, with the result that his angels are unmistakable Angels, and not mere copies of those of Boucher, Bartolozzi, or Kauffmann. They were usually painted in rose or crimson camaieu,[2] and no two are alike; they are boldly and freely drawn, flying or resting upon clouds, sketched in swift outline and then filled in with the full brush with no stippling or hatching of any sort [110]. The obvious spontaneity of drawing of these charming little beings is lacking in Askew's ordinary figure subjects, although his colours are always good and his attention to detail much more pronounced, probably because he was copying from engravings.[3] Another class of paintings of children, sheep, and other rustic or pastoral subjects[4] is probably attributable to Askew's son, Robert.

In common with the painters of other factories those of Derby were sometimes called upon to decorate replacements to services made elsewhere, and Major Tapp has pointed out that some of this sort of work was probably done by Fidelle Duvivier, who had painted fables at Chelsea[5] before he was engaged by Duesbury in 1769. It is at any rate certain that many accomplished figure subjects are to be seen on early Derby wares [136], which from their general style, common use of brick-red rocks in the foreground, distant mauve hills, and foliage in green, brown, and yellow (with no glaring contrasts) may be credited to the same artist.

The name of James Banford, the landscape artist, occurs many times in the pattern books as a figure painter, which might be expected from the fact that his work was invariably in miniature style. For this reason his portraits of girls and his classical or symbolical subjects are painted most carefully with elaborate attention to detail, in subdued but harmonizing colours, on small cabinet pieces.[6] The work of the Brewers[7] is almost equally fine and delicate, and both worked in the modern style with wiped-out highlights and a liberal use of the opaque chrome green.

[1]Herbert Allen Collection, no 49; Schreiber Collection, pl 47, no 398.
[2]Old English Porcelain, Honey, pl 41B. [3]Old Derby Porcelain, Hurlbutt, pls 36, 37, 39 and 44.
[4]Old English Porcelain, Honey, pl 45b; V. & A. Museum, no 3038–1901.
[5]Jefferyes Hamett O'Neale, Tapp, pl 29.
[6]Old Derby Porcelain, Hurlbutt, pls 40–41; Old English Porcelain, Honey, pl 44a; Crown Derby Porcelain, Gilhespy, fig 44. [7]Old Derby Porcelain, Hurlbutt, pls 42–43.

An unbroken succession of figure painters worked at Derby until the closure. Cuthbert Lawton is famed for his animal painting,[1] and his name has been suggested as the author of spirited hunting scenes[2] which are more properly to be credited to a contemporary named William Cotton, who left Derby in 1821 for the Potteries. Then came William Cordon (or Corden), the landscape painter, who supplemented his income by painting portraits on porcelain, and William Dixon, who according to Haslem copied Hogarthian subjects from prints by John Collier (alias 'Tim Bobbin'), in bright enamels on a large scale,[3] subjects more curious and amusing than beautiful. Last within the scope of our period is William Watson, whose work in gold on a light or dark blue ground[4] has a distinct kinship with the Chamberlain vermilion bottles and the Spode matt gilding on a claret ground.

Figure painting was not developed at Coalport until after 1850, by which time the imitation of Sèvres shapes and decoration had reached its peak. In the French style we may see numerous copies of Boucher's subjects,[5] classical ones in monochrome,[6] and Cupids in cameo relief style which are lifeless compared with those of Askew. They were probably painted by William Cook, who did the same sort of work at Madeley,[7] although R. F. Abraham, who left to go to Copelands as Art Director, is credited with a similar style.

Practically the whole of the Nantgarw figure painting was done in London, the only noteworthy exception being a few countryside scenes[8] drawn probably from memory by Thomas Pardoe, usually featuring rustics. The artists employed by John Simms were undoubtedly responsible for most of the finer work, and among them was James Plant, who painted landscapes and figures.[9] Binns says that he worked at Chamberlains before he went to London, and Haslem refers to his painting as being 'probably the best things ever done on china; among them were several charming groups of children.' This clue helps to identify a series of groups of children, often winged like cupids, and either enclosed in cages or else resting on 'inverted bonnets trimmed with ribbons' (John). The same artist was perhaps responsible for the more mundane groups of children at play. Charles Muss was another London artist, who worked first at Coalport before joining his father's studio. His work is reputed to have consisted of landscapes and figures rendered in sepia and purple monochrome. John Martin worked for the same elder Muss, and since he was celebrated in another sphere as a painter of Biblical subjects in oil it is probable that the unidentified classical scenes sometimes seen on Nantgarw porcelain might have been done by him.

[1]*Old Derby Porcelain*, Hurlbutt, pl 38. [2]*Crown Derby Porcelain*. Gilhespy, figs 69 and 70. [3]*Ibid*, figs 82–83. [4]*Ibid*, figs 84 and 85. [5]Barrett, figs 126 and 144. [6]*Idem*, fig 140. [7]*Idem*, figs 161 and 162. [8]*Nantgarw Porcelain*, John, pl 57. [9]*Ibid*, pl 33*a* and *b*.

Apart from the numerous Oriental styles hardly any figure painting was done at Plymouth and Bristol. The early sauce-boats and vases are very rarely painted with insignificant, crudely drawn figures in rustic dress against sketchy landscape backgrounds, and at a later date figures were occasionally painted as tours-de-force on specially made services. Most well known of these is the 'Parliamentary Service' which was produced to serve as evidence for the Committee formed to decide upon an extension of Cookworthy's patent, which had been transferred to Champion. The inevitable green festoons enclose paintings of the Metamorphoses of Ovid, *en grisaille* on a Pompeian-red ground,[2] while a service made by Champion for presentation to Mrs Burke on the occasion of her husband's return to Parliament is painted with symbolical figures supporting a coat-of-arms.[3] The date of these services is approximately the same, but they were rare exceptions and may in no way be looked upon as representative factory decoration.

In this, as in so many another branch of decoration, the Potteries followed the lead of Worcester and Derby, and little was produced which is either outstanding or novel. When figure painting is seen at all, which is rarely, it is usually well done [114 & 115], whether it be on a scale suited to the favourite mantelpiece vases[4] or whether restricted to smaller cabinet pieces.[5]

[1]*Cookworthy's Plymouth and Bristol Porcelain*, Mackenna, figs 38 and 39.
[2]*Bristol Porcelain*, Hurlbutt, pl 35. [3]*Ibid*, pl 36a. [4]*Spode and his Successors*, Hayden, frontispiece.
[5]*Ibid*, opp p 124.

CHAPTER ELEVEN

Heraldic Painting

It was the common custom during the first half of the 18th century for services bearing coats-of-arms and crests to be made in China to the order of wealthy English families. So far as similar decoration in this country is concerned the 'Chinese Lowestoft' myth is best forgotten, but at the same time a certain amount of heraldic painting was done at several of the fritt-paste factories, though never on a large scale. The intention was invariably to decorate single specimens, probably for presentation purposes, rather than to attempt the making of entire services.

At Bow [123],[1] in keeping with the typical inconsistency of that factory's decoration, designs were occasionally made up of heraldry and Kakiemon motifs,[2] though to be quite fair it must be acknowledged that similar incongruities are to be seen on Chinese wares of the same class and period. Heraldry was seldom painted on Chelsea porcelain,[3] but upon that of Worcester it is comparatively common, doubtless because noble patronage was enjoyed from the very beginning. Coats-of-arms are seldom seen as the sole decoration, but are incorporated, often inconspicuously, into whatever style of painting was in vogue at the particular time. Thus, while the Meissen influence was predominant in the 1760s the painters combined heraldry with landscapes in colours and in lilac monochrome, with flowers and with considerable scroll-work in gold or puce.[4] Later, in the 1770s, the Sèvres fashion brought with it coloured borders, gilt dentil edges, floral festoons, and the use of the effective Worcester 'dry blue'.[5]

The decoration of services in armorial style was undertaken at Bristol, where Champion made a practice of making tea-services for presentation to influential people [124 & 125]. His predecessor, Cookworthy, had on rare occasion produced isolated pieces similar to those made elsewhere,[6] but the new departure resulted in wares which are among the most attractive (while yet still typically Bristol) of English

[1]Figures within brackets refer to plates at the back of this book.
[2]*Old English Porcelain*, Honey, pl 26c; Schreiber Collection, pl 10, no 79.
[3]Schreiber Collection, pl 45, no 387.
[4]Frank Lloyd Collection, pl 80, nos 385 and 388, pl 82, nos 386 and 387; *Worcester Porcelain*, Barrett, pls 46–47. [5]*Ibid*, pl 83, nos 389 and 390; Schreiber Collection, pl 64, no 523.
[6]*Cookworthy's Plymouth and Bristol Porcelain*, Mackenna, pl 3.

94

'hard paste' porcelains. The festoons, sprays, and gilded borders have already been described, but in this connexion it is interesting to note that Dr Mackenna has suggested that even the formal Tudor rose from which festoons so often depend may have an heraldic significance, since Champion's own arms included a spray of three such blooms, a motif which is indeed often seen in the decoration of his porcelain. What is probably the best known of these tea-services, made for the Burkes, has already been mentioned, and in addition there is the Chough service, in which the little Cornish bird is a perfect foil to the festoons,[1] and the Edwards,[2] similar in conception but somewhat less carefully painted.

Such beginnings led to a riotous outbreak of heraldry in the 19th century, notably at Worcester, Rockingham, and Stoke-on-Trent. By and large it was a vulgar manifestation of the love for colour of that time, especially at Worcester, where elaborate coats-of-arms, overpowering enough in themselves, were sometimes allied to the most intricate and gaudy Japan patterns to cover the entire surface of every piece. As Mr Hobson has pointed out, it is really better to remove decoration from the gravy and to relegate it to the rim, and the most pleasing of all heraldic painting is that in which the white paste is undecorated save for a tiny but well-painted crest on a gadrooned, gilt-edged rim. Many Worcester services were treated in this way, and almost equally effective, despite the problem of the gravy, is the placing of a small crest in the centre, in conjunction with a wide, coloured border [129]. The heraldic painter, Plant, was responsible for the best of these services, his style is that of the miniature painter, and his figure work is particularly detailed and correct [128]. Both Flights and Chamberlains made countless large services for the wealthy and for the London Companies,[3] and there is little to choose between their products, though those of the latter factory tend always to be more ornate and elaborate, particularly as regards the gadrooned borders, which are often painted in Japan, arabesque, or geometrical design.

At a time when survival depended on patronage the future of many a factory was staked on the making of this sort of ware. For such as Worcester, possessing large resources, experience, and London showrooms there was no problem, as we may see from a study of the Catalogue of the Worcester Works Museum, which lists upwards of forty services made for outstanding people or companies, apart from scores of others from which specimens still survive. Every royal visit, with its entourage, meant new orders, and every country squire followed suit. Josiah Spode II, ever anxious to outdo his Worcester rivals, found his perfected felspar porcelain eminently suited for

---

[1]*Champion's Bristol Porcelain*, Mackenna, fig 75. [2]*Ibid*, fig 77.
[3]Herbert Allen Collection, pl 62, no 307.

armorial wares [126], [1] for it was white enough to flatter his good colours and durable enough to preserve them. On the other hand, when the Rockingham factory closed in 1842, its downfall was partly if not wholly due to the attempted manufacture, in 1830, of an enormous and magnificent service to the order of William IV. In this class of decoration, as in others, extreme emphasis on colour and gold, and the technical ability to make the most of them, led inevitably to disaster.

[1]*Spode and his Successors*, Hayden, opp p 142.

CHAPTER TWELVE

Gilding

Gilding has been applied to porcelain since the days when the Chinese used it upon what was in their eyes one of the rarest and most lovely of man-made substances. This they did sparingly, tastefully, and so did our early porcelain makers, though the tendency to use gold as a decoration in itself gradually became more pronounced, to culminate unfortunately in late 19th-century specimens in which the entire surface of the ware was gilded, and all the character lost of the underlying white body. In this country gilding has taken many forms, but we shall mention only those in which pure gold has been used, since it is well known that baser metals have sometimes been used to give similar though much inferior effects.

The simplest, though not necessarily the earliest form of gilding was that in which gold leaf was fixed to the ware with oil or japanners' size, just as it is still applied by the picture framer or the house decorator. It was unfired, and, of course, it did not long withstand rough usage or repeated washing. For this reason, although William Littler undoubtedly made extensive use of it at Longton Hall it is rarely seen on his porcelain, and there is a considerable class of specimens painted in Littler's Blue on which the remaining traces of it give but a hint of original splendour.

At the same time other factories with greater resources were able to use the more durable and attractive 'honey gilding', as it is called. Gold leaf was mixed with honey, painted on, and fired, giving a dull gold which could be burnished with a bloodstone and chased with a metal point. Sometimes a lead-glass flux was included in the mixture, though this was not essential since the gold would normally adhere to the body through the fusing of the glaze. Honey gilding is seen at its best upon the early 'soft' pastes such as those of Sèvres, Chelsea, and Worcester, because of the soft richness of their glazes; a 'hard' body usually accompanies a thin glaze, with a resultant thin gilding, and vice versa, although Bristol gold is exceptionally fine despite the 'hard' paste beneath it. This is the reason why Chelsea gilding, though sparingly used as a rule, is of such excellent quality, so that it could be used to good effect as a pigment on the wonderful mazarine and gold specimens already mentioned.[1] Worcester gilding carried on where Chelsea left off, and it has never been surpassed either

[1] *Old English Porcelain*, Honey, pls 15 and 16.

in quality or in the ways in which it was used. Scrollwork, foliage, lace-work, and other designs of all sorts were delicately drawn [1] in conjunction with coloured grounds or scale patterns. During the last few years of the Wall period gold was used in dainty floral bouquets and sprigs on the white body, with no other form of decoration. Sometimes, when a raised effect was required, at Worcester and elsewhere, the gold was applied over an undercoating of fired enamel, usually vermilion or crimson, but sometimes yellow or orange, or else was mixed with such a pigment and fired in one operation. The latter was a cheaper process, and gave a rather colder and duller effect. The burnishing and chasing which was the final process was (and, of course, still is) an extremely skilled craft, on whatever sort of gilding. The burnishing was done with bloodstones (or agates) fixed in wooden handles, and the necessary vigorous rubbing was applied through a linen cloth, after which the gold was cleaned with a mixture of vinegar and white lead. By this means lovely effects of contrasting dull and bright gold could be obtained, as we may see on much Bristol porcelain, when a border may have an inner dull band between two burnished ones, or be divided diagonally in the same contrasting manner. The chasing was done with a metal point, by which means all sorts of designs could be drawn upon the dull or shining surface.

One might almost say that Worcester, with Chelsea, had a virtual monopoly of fine gilding during the 1760s. The Bow gold, though pleasantly soft, was not of the highest quality and it was used sparingly. At Lowestoft, gilding was hardly used at all, save as an enamel in certain slight sprig and diaper patterns, with black. [2] Some blue borders rather crudely 'marbled' in gold, in imitation of a Sèvres and Worcester style, are characteristic of at least one of the Liverpool factories, [3] the bright, thin gilding of so much Caughley 'blue-and-white' [4] was almost certainly added outside the factory, and at Derby very few early pieces had any gold upon them. Bristol gold was naturally used mainly with the characteristic flower painting, usually either in complex foliate scrolls and panels of close trellis diaper, [5] or with the typical festoons which often hang from gold rosettes or are looped into gold lines. A style common to Bristol, Chelsea, and Worcester takes the form of curving radial gold lines, forming a ground for floral bouquets, and borders may be either single gold lines or dentil edging in several forms, notably 'saw-tooth' or semi-oval, outside or inside the rim, or both.

The introduction of mercury-amalgam gilding took place about 1790. It was a new, easier process, and it rapidly superseded the old, though its results are brassier and harder. The mercury with which the gold is blended vapourizes in the kiln, leaving

[1] *Ibid*, pls 70, 75, and 76. [2] *Old English Porcelain*, Honey, pl 54b. [3] Schreiber Collection, pl 88, no 783. [4] Barrett, fig 46. [5] *Champion's Bristol Porcelain*, Mackenna, fig 2.

behind a dull surface which needs burnishing to a greater or lesser degree. Thus, some of the more expensive later Worcester wares, for example, have as many as eight concentric border patterns, some flat and some raised, some burnished to a pale brilliance, some glowing dully, and some almost matt, and with delicate tooling applied to them all [128]. [1] At the same factory this later gilding was used to give quite a new appearance to the wide-deep blue borders of some of the old patterns, and for various forms of gold vermiculation [2] or sea-weed pattern on both coloured and white grounds. Coalport gilding is usually thin and highly burnished, which fact helps to distinguish copies of Meissen, Sèvres, and Chelsea from the originals, while a common doubt as to a Coalport or Rockingham provenance may often be decided by the more coppery tone of the gilding of the latter factory. Swansea and Nantgarw gilding is of course of the highest quality, though it is liable to considerable tarnishing.

The marked colourfulness of the porcelain made under Josiah Spode II, even in an age of colour, is due in no small measure to lavishness of gilding. Church, writing many years ago, described Spode gold as being 'of great solidity and smoothness, quite the best of his day', and he probably referred to its introduction, about 1802, in a dead matt form, on large surfaces such as plinths, handles, and knobs. This fashion was entirely new, although it was actually inspired by the ormolu mounts so beloved at Sèvres, and it is credited to Henry Daniell, the chief enameller and gilder of the time. Otherwise, in its flat, burnished form, it was used generally in floral or foliate scrolls, or in arabesque patterns, looking at its best (as indeed all gilding does) upon dark blue grounds. We have already mentioned the amazingly delicate bat-printing in gold upon a dark mazarine ground which was another Spode speciality, and the designs in matt gold on a maroon ground which were attempts to imitate lacquer. It is perhaps unfortunate that Josiah II was bound to pander to the newly-rich in their demand for over-elaboration in gilding as well as colour, with the result that the perfect surface of his improved porcelain bodies was sometimes entirely hidden. As we have pointed out in a previous chapter the same criticism may be made of the later Derby Japans, whose superfluity of gilding makes them vastly inferior to the earlier, more restrained examples.

[1]Figures within brackets refer to plates at the back of this book.
[2]*Old English Porcelain*, Honey, pl 78c.

CHAPTER THIRTEEN

Outside Decoration

In previous chapters continual reference has been made to the fact that much of our early porcelain was decorated outside the factory walls. Either their proprietors could afford to pay for the services of skilled independent painters, or else their wares were good enough to sell readily to dealers or to decorating establishments, while still in the undecorated or partially decorated state. In the course of this short chapter, which can be little more than an introduction to such a large subject, many familiar names will be encountered, names of those who worked as studio artists from the beginning or who received their training as decorators at one of the factories before leaving to better themselves at an established firm of specialists. In both classes must be included those who had no stock-in-trade other than their skill, and who were supplied with piece-work which could afterwards be fired in the factory kilns.

No name is more familiar to collectors than that of James Giles, who is listed in Mortimer's Directory for 1763 as a 'China and Enamel Painter, Berwick Street, Soho', and who himself advertised four years later that he had perfected enamelling 'for many years'. It would seem that he had other premises in Kentish Town from 1760 to 1763, and in Cockspur Street, Charing Cross, from 1767 to 1776, but about 1778, according to the reliable Jewitt, 'on the failure of Giles' the business was taken over by Duesbury. Our information concerning him is derived from two main sources, the advertisements which he published from time to time, and the various account books which he left behind. In the latter regard we learn that he painted porcelain for Duesbury, Philip Christian of Liverpool, William Davis & Co of Worcester, Turner of Caughley, and numerous London dealers. From the same source comes the information that in 1773 he bought engraved copper plates from 'Thomas Turner of Worcester', that by far the greater part of his painting was done on white or 'blue-and-white' Worcester porcelain, and that apart from his work as a decorator he was also a dealer who sold Worcester and Derby wares on a fifteen per cent commission basis. The period covered by the books, that is from 1771 to 1776, naturally tells us nothing about the earlier years during which he painted on Bow, Chelsea, and Longton Hall wares.

'Decorated by Giles' does not, of course, mean that all the painting was done by

Giles himself, for he is known to have employed many decorators, including such skilled artists as Richard Dyer and even O'Neale himself, the master of them all. The work done included many types of subject – figures, flowers, fruit, coloured grounds, and fine gilding, according to the advertisements, but pride of place must undoubtedly be given to the famous 'exotic birds' which have already been fully described. Some years ago Mr Honey gave considerable thought to English bird painting on Chinese porcelain, not birds of the 'dishevelled' type, but those which are boldly rendered in a 'wet' style with a full brush. He found the same characteristics on both Chelsea and Worcester wares, and he came to the conclusion that the work was done by an outside decorator, probably employed by Giles. Furthermore, a comparison between other Chinese and English pieces suggested a similar outside origin for the 'dishevelled' bird. In the former regard Mr Honey discovered some plates in the possession of a Miss Grubbe, which had traditionally been made for the occasion of the wedding of an ancestor by a 'John Giles', and which were painted in the 'wet' style with the typical closely packed foliage in the foreground and the thick gilding which invariably accompany it. Since both Jewitt and Binns have confused the names of John and James there is no need to be sidetracked by a similar error here, and we should next consider the possible identity of this particular employee. Pieces are known of Worcester and Chelsea origin which show the same unmistakable sureness of touch and the same mannerisms, and it is possible that the unknown artist may have worked at Chelsea before and at Worcester after he worked at the studio. Binns mentions Dyer as well as Williman and Mills as having worked at Chelsea; the Bowcocke papers record that Dyer worked at 'Mr Bolton's, enameler, the Church, Lambeth', and it is more than probable that Giles may have taken over these premises, together with those employed thereat, when he set up in business. There then is a tentative suggestion, that Dyer may have been the 'wet' painter of birds, figures, and fruit.

So far as the 'dishevelled' birds are concerned there can be no success in an attempt to identify their author by name. His style, with its curious hatching in parallel lines, characteristic leaves in the foreground, and ground like 'a handful of wet hay' (to quote Mr Rackham) is to be seen on Bow wares as well as on those of Chelsea and Worcester, and his style is evident also in fruit and flower painting, as well as in such armorial work as the Blackshame arms on a tea-pot in the Schreiber Collection.

In 1768 Giles advertised as 'China and Enamel Painter' and as 'Proprietor of the Worcester Porcelaine Warehouse', and that he had a 'great variety of white goods by him' to be painted to customers' orders in 'any pattern they shall chuse'. To this effrontery Worcester replied, describing their own goods and referring to 'some of their ware . . . advertised at another Room, painted in London'. Thereafter Giles dropped his misleading claim. It would appear that though he was not official enameller to the works as he at first pretended, this disagreement in no way affected his supplies, which he painted with the enamel colours he had brought to 'great perfection' and which he was willing to sell to the trade. A ledger entry under 'Philip Christian & Sons', dated 28th February 1776 reads 'by cash in full by Enamel Colours sold on self acct. £14–11–6'. Among partly decorated wares bought from Worcester were those printed in overglaze black and lilac, to which he added slight coloured decoration in the well-known style [137].[1] Nightingale records that such a lot of 'jet enamelled' ware was bought by him at the 1769 sale, and in addition the fact that he bought copper plates points to the probability that on occasion he did his own printing, which, of course, he was well equipped to do. We should distinguish between Giles' overpainted transfers and certain Worcester designs such as the well-known 'red bull', in which the colour is an inherent part of the design, to be applied within the factory.

With regard to Bow the Bowcocke papers include receipted bills from Dyer, 'at Mr Bolton's enameler', and the same source refers to 'bisket ware made at New Canton', inferring that such was made to be sold in the undecorated state. It is moreover significant that though factory site excavations have unearthed much unfired blue-painted ware, very little enamelled has been found. Who, then, painted upon the more ambitious pieces? Specimens are known which are characteristic of O'Neale's style,[2] but who is to say that he did not work at Bow? On the other hand, as Mr Honey has pointed out, both Giles and the Bow proprietors received financial aid from Duesbury before he took over their businesses, and he may well have brought them together for their (and for his) mutual advantage. If this were indeed so, there might be an explanation of the occurrence of Giles painting on anchor/dagger marked pieces, though if, as has been suggested, such a mark was applied by Giles as his own mark one would have expected to find it upon wares made at other factories.

Giles's ledgers are unfortunately too late to supply any description of his work at Chelsea, and it is possible only to say that the 'fruit painter' may have worked with him. The absence on Derby porcelain of any of the styles favoured at his establishment indicates that his retirement in 1778 was a permanent one.

Some of the finest work on porcelain was done by Jefferyes Hamett O'Neale, whose career covers a period from about 1750 to 1775, but whose movements, despite

[1]Figures within brackets refer to plates at the back of this book.
[2]*Old English Porcelain*, Honey, pl 34.

exhaustive research by Major Tapp, remain somewhat of a mystery. His earlier painting,[1] which includes many of the 'Fable paintings' for which he is best known, is found on Chelsea porcelain [131–133]. The direct inspiration of the fable subjects came from Francis Barlow's *Fables*, published in 1687, though the same tales had been the subject of Ogilby's *Fables of Aesop paraphrased in verse*, which was published in 1651. O'Neale painted them in colour or in monochrome, and the fact that his signature occasionally appears in a hidden form on both Chelsea and Worcester specimens helps to pin down his distinctive style, though among those who copied it accurately were the accomplished Duviviers. There is evidence to show that O'Neale lived in Worcester from 1767 to 1769, but nothing to show that he was ever a factory artist. Indeed, since some of his Worcester work is signed[2] it is almost certain that he worked at home, since signatures were forbidden to the factory decorators. From September 1770 to 1771 he was at Wedgwoods, for there was correspondence concerning him between Wedgwood and his partner, Bentley, which indicates the high esteem in which he was regarded. His work at Etruria was rather in the sphere of preparing designs which could be repeated on a commercial scale[3] than of actually painting on the ware, and this was, of course, in keeping with Josiah's outlook, which demanded beauty and utility for everybody rather than for the wealthy few. From 1771 until about 1773 O'Neale was back at Chelsea, whence he moved to one or other of the decorating studios. To which it is impossible to say, though his work[4] is to be seen on porcelain made as late as the 1780s.

The fable subjects merit a short description, for they are outstandingly beautiful and interesting. The animals are invariably full of life,[5] whether they be real or mythical, usually with swollen joints and with red, protruding tongues; figures are always correct, though often incongruously clothed, as in classical subjects which are peopled with long-bodied peasants in brilliant blue, carmine, and pink dress. Landscapes have blue rivers with divided waterfalls, punt-like boats, and brown or vandyke rocks in the near foreground. Trees are shaded in horizontal lines, often realistically split, broken, or gnarled, with an occasional contrasting slender birch with separate green or red leaves, or a row of stumpy poplars. Larger trees are sometimes bent over as by a prevailing wind, with their colours applied in long, curling brush-strokes in contrasting reds and greens. O'Neale never used yellow in his foliage, at least on English wares. His classical subjects commonly include ruins and broken obelisks, with lichen hanging from them, and urns drawn purposely out of proportion. Large banks of blue

[1] *Jefferyes Hamett O'Neale*, Tapp, figs 28, 29, 50, 51, 56, 62. [2] *Ibid*, figs 10–13.
[3] *Ibid*, figs 63–65. [4] *Ibid*, figs 66 and 66a.
[5] Frank Lloyd Collection, pl 75, nos 351 and 352, pl 81, no 352A; *Worcester Porcelain*, Barrett, pls 81–83.

or mauve cumulus cloud lower above blue or puce hills, never mauve, and in the skies are flocks of small, high-flying birds.

It is probable that O'Neale studied at Chelsea under a certain William Duvivier, who died in 1775. This skilled painter from Tournai was almost certainly the originator of the fable subjects, and he also taught his son and his nephew, Fidelle and Joseph Michel, the former coming to Chelsea in 1764 to replace Joseph who had left to return to France, and taking employment under Duesbury in 1769. Joseph's work, which like that of Fidelle is very similar to that of O'Neale, is, of course, found only on Chelsea and Tournai wares,[1] and differs from it only in small detail – whereas the Englishman was a devotee of the full brush Joseph preferred to obtain his shades of colour with coarse stippling, which he used for the foliage of his trees. Fidelle, on the other hand, is known to have stayed in this country for over twenty years, during which time he painted at many factories in a style which changed with the passing years. At first, at Chelsea, only slight differences in palette distinguish his work[2] from O'Neale's – he used a bright yellow for his leaves, which O'Neale never did – but a simple style was not well suited to the pieces he was called upon to decorate under Duesbury's direction, and he seems to have developed a style of figure painting, sometimes classical but leaning more and more towards the rustic, which features large, boldly painted figures in a palette predominantly reddish-brown, blue, and green. Major Tapp has traced his later career through many factories, including Caughley (1773–4) [130], Lane End (1789), and New Hall,[3] with a brief interlude in his native country, at Sceaux, in 1775. In addition, his hand is to be seen on Derby porcelain [136], even upon Worcester, for Mr T. G. Burn has a lovely pair of cabbage-leaf jugs, painted with large figure subjects in a style which is almost certainly his.

Very little is known of John Donaldson, whose painting upon Worcester porcelain of the 1760s is among the finest of its kind.[4] Redgrave tells us that he was born in Edinburgh in 1737, and we gather that he first became known as a skilled miniature painter in Indian ink, and that he became a member of the Incorporated Society of Artists by virtue of his fame as a portrait painter, presumably in colours. The same writer states that he painted on Worcester porcelain sent to him in London, though this possibility is clearly subject to the same objections which have already been put forward. Wherever his work was done, whether in a decorating studio, at his London home, or in a factory, his style is unmistakable. He painted rather blowsy figures with unnaturally bright cheeks, in the French manner of Boucher,[5] which have a distinct

[1] *Jefferyes Hamett O'Neale*, Tapp, figs 58, 59 and 62A. [2] *Ibid*, Tapp, fig 35 and 57.
[3] *19th Century English Pottery and Porcelain*, Bemrose, pl 9B. [4] Frank Lloyd Collection, pl 76, no 353.
[5] *Worcester Porcelain*, Hobson, pls LXXV, LXXIX, LXXXI and LXXXII.

family likeness to those in an engraving by J. Finlason of 'The Newsmongers by Donaldson', dated 1st May 1769. He also painted children with plump faces and limbs in a more intimate manner which was probably the style of his miniature portrait painting [135].

Apart from these outstanding artists there must have been countless other early decorators about whom nothing is known, though indeed a handful of names has survived, names such as Robert Allen, manager of Lowestoft in 1780 and afterwards proprietor of a local studio, Absolon of Yarmouth, Thomas Hughes of Clerkenwell, and William Kempson and John Bolton of Kentish Town. Their styles have not been identified, and since most of them were free-lance workers their painting is likely to be seen on many sorts of porcelain and pottery. The only name which is outstanding among such as these (and that only because of later associations) is that of William Duesbury who, before launching out as a manufacturer, painted on salt-glaze and on the porcelains of Bow, Chelsea, Derby, and Staffordshire. We know this because of an existing work book for the years 1751–3, but specimens of his brushwork are rare. [1]

Round about the turn of the century, at a time when good porcelain could be made quicker than it could be painted (at least without the employment of a large staff of artists), there were many large enamelling establishments, most of them in London. Some of them have already been mentioned and can now be described in fuller detail. In the V. & A. Museum there is a painting by Thomas Baxter [2] of his father's studio at no 1, Gough Street, where the porcelain of Worcester, Caughley, and Coalport, was decorated. Richard Robins and T. Martin Randall has a similar business in Spa Fields, Islington, and specialized in the finishing of Swansea and Nantgarw from about 1810 to 1830. Robins had learnt his trade at Pinxton, Randall at Caughley and Derby, and both were working partners, though the latter is better known for his Madeley birds and coloured grounds. Moses Webster was employed there between 1819 and 1822, probably as a flower painter on the white Sèvres which had been obtained when the French factory finally abandoned the *pâte tendre* in 1813. It is well known that Randall's successful decoration of Minton wares in French style led to his being offered a partnership, which his age led him to decline.

It has been stressed that the Derby concern was a prolific source of the supply of artists to the entire ceramic industry of the early 19th century. John Simms worked under Duesbury II as a flower painter, and began work on his own account in Pimlico in 1792, in partnership with his son William. Among their artists was Zachariah Boreman, who painted the landscapes, and James Turner, who was responsible for

[1]*Old English Porcelain*, Honey, pl 25*b*; Schreiber Collection, pl 10, no 36.
[2]*Porcelain*, Dillon, pl 47.

many of the fine roses painted on Nantgarw porcelain.[1] The figures and miniatures were done by James Plant,[2] who went there in 1803 from Chamberlains.

The firm of Muss and Son, Bonifacio and Charles, had premises in Great Windmill Street. Charles worked under Rose at Coalport as a landscape and figure painter, both in polychrome and in sepia and purple monochrome, though he is probably best known for his documentary view of the Coalport factory. Familiar names among their workmen are John Martin, the supposed painter of classical scenes[3] on Nantgarw and Worcester porcelain, and Silk, the Caughley landscape painter. In addition to these more important establishments Haslem lists those of Cartwright & Son, Anderson, and Battam as being those responsible for the best decoration of the period 1810–30, decoration which for the most part outclassed that of any contemporary factory with the possible exception of Spode. The muffle kilns which were used to fire the decoration are reputed to have been heated by charcoal, and the pigments, by virtue of their highly alkaline nature, were fired at a temperature lower than that used in the factories. Undecorated wares were supplied to them either by the makers or by the London china dealers, and they sometimes bought their own supplies, as did Giles at an earlier date.

Among the dealers the name of Mortlock, of Orchard Street and Oxford Street, was for many years supreme, from the beginning in 1746 to comparatively recent times. John Mortlock & Co dealt almost exclusively in expensive, lavishly decorated porcelain, which they supplied to the nobility and even to royalty; not only did they buy white porcelain which they sent out to be painted, but they were agents for such firms as Coalport, Worcester, Rockingham, and Swansea. Much London decorated Nantgarw ware was undoubtedly finished to their orders; it was bought in the white and painted in Sèvres style to meet the demand for French porcelain. Binns says that Mortlock 'contracted to take the whole of the ware in the white state', and although much of it would bear the impressed mark it is nevertheless likely that some of it was bought as genuine Sèvres. It is, of course, perfectly obvious that Billingsley's experiments in Wales were dictated throughout by the exacting requirements of the London dealers.

The free-lance decorator had need to be exceptionally talented to hold his own among the many studios, both in this country and elsewhere. James Donovan & Son of Dublin, for example, had a considerable trade with the English factories, notably with Mintons, and like others they did not hesitate to claim through their marks that they were the actual manufacturers. Billingsley could stand in any company, and his

[1]*Nantgarw Porcelain*, John, coloured illustrations, 11b and 29b. [2]*Ibid*, pl 33a.
[3]Herbert Allen Collection, no 312.

work at Mansfield and Torksey was probably confined almost if not entirely to the painting of porcelain made by others. [1] His rival and contemporary, Thomas Pardoe, worked in Bristol upon the stock of white Nantgarw left behind when Billingsley and Walker left for Coalport in 1820, which he painted with flowers, fruit, butterflies, birds, animals, shells, and landscapes. It is equally as difficult to identify his work as it is to pin down the brushwork of so many others who have been mentioned. There is no doubt that there was always a large number of artists working outside, at home and in studios, whose names are unrecorded, but who have left behind them so much to be treasured and admired.

[1]*Pottery and Porcelain of Swansea and Nantgarw*, Nance, pl xcix; *Nantgarw Porcelain*, John, pl 37a.

CHAPTER FOURTEEN

Final Words

It has been said more than once that the history of potting is the history of mankind. Certainly it is true that the services of the artist in clay have always been indispensable to man. In the more restricted sphere of the decoration upon the clay – for the finest porcelain is little more – it is surely equally true to say that in it is mirrored the ever-changing outlook and taste of our people, or at any rate of those who had an interest in the cultural side of everyday life.

The debt owed to the Chinese by our 18th-century ancestors is sometimes under-rated, for though Eastern art was reproduced in many branches of craftsmanship it was through the medium of porcelain that it became familiar to the man-in-the-street, even though the likeness was sometimes sadly distorted. The gulf between earthenware and porcelain was bridged in a remarkably short space of time, par-ticularly as regards the decoration upon them, but as soon as the passage was effected there was an overwhelming awakening of interest in things foreign, particularly in those from the East. There was an almost insatiable demand for the clean-looking, thin wares, blue painted or printed in Chinese style, which the factories were quickly able to supply. At the same time, in the homes of the wealthy the 'Chinese Chippen-dale' furnishings were enhanced by the polychrome English versions of the powder-blue, the *'famille-rose'*, and the *'famille verte'*; it was an ancient civilization which was leavening English life, but a wholesome and above all an artistic one. Apart from the natural transition to the designs of Meissen and Sèvres, as these porcelains found their way into the country, there was I think a further expansion of the same striving towards graceful living. It was, too, a very popular striving, since porcelain was by that time within the reach of all but the very poorest, and the love of beauty which characterized the late 18th century was furthered in no small measure by the ceramic artist. The 'middle class' could not afford or appreciate the Chelsea figures and 'toys' of the wealthy, but the transfer-printed Spode copies of Chinese porcelain were well within their reach. The gaudy nature of much early 19th-century decoration, too, was a reflection of an age when many a sudden rise to affluence outstepped the good taste which ideally should have kept pace with it, while still later an unfortunate emphasis on meaningless ornament allied to an absence of true beauty of form typified the worst aspect of Victorian craftsmanship and outlook.

At the present day we are in the fortunate position of being able to turn over a new leaf and to start afresh. The restrictions of wartime enforced simplicity, and undecorated wares were often perforce so well shaped as to render ornamentation superfluous. The potter was obliged to study form because colour was denied to him, while at the same time this paucity of colour rekindled public interest in the designs of the past. With the end of restrictions there are signs that the virtues of restraint in decoration are fully appreciated. The painters of the early days were so prolific of ideas that few possibilities were ignored, and while many modern designers have recognized that reproductions of their work are worthwhile and acceptable, others are carrying on that tradition of simple treatment of natural motifs which is so well suited to porcelain.

In conclusion, I would urge that my reader should lose no opportunity of seeing the originals of such specimens as those which are illustrated in these pages. There is no lack of them in the public collections and in the private houses which are open to view, and neither monochrome nor coloured plates can do full justice to a beauty which has matured with the passing years.

BIBLIOGRAPHY

There can never be a thoroughly up-to-date bibliography of English Porcelain, and any attempt to compile a complete one would fill a large volume. I have selected the following from the great mass of literature on the subject, omitting books published in foreign languages, and including only those which are moderately priced. Many are out-of-date but still valuable for our purpose by reason of their illustrations. Books to which reference is made in the text are marked with an asterisk, and it is important to note that some of them have extended to more than one edition, with resultant changes in page and plate numbers.

General

BURTON W. *Porcelain: its nature, art, and Manufacture* 1906

DILLON E. *Porcelain* 1904

HONEY W.B. *Art of the Potter* 1946; *European Ceramic Art* 1949*

Oriental

BRITISH MUSEUM *Guide to the Pottery and Porcelain of the East* 1924; *Handbook of the Pottery and Porcelain of the Far East* 1937

GULLAND W.G. *Chinese Porcelain* (5th Ed, 2 vols) 1928

HOBSON R.L. *Chinese Pottery and Porcelain* (2 vols) 1915; *Later Ceramic Wares of China* 1925; *Wares of the Ming Dynasty* 1923

HONEY W.B. *Ceramic Art of China and other countries of the Far East* 1945

Continental

AUSCHER E.S. *History and Description of French Porcelain* 1905

FRANTZ H. *French Pottery and Porcelain* 1906

HONEY W.B. *Dresden China* 1947; *French Porcelain of the 18th Century* 1950; *German Porcelain* 1947

English

BARRETT F. A. *Caughley and Coalport Porcelain* 1951*; *Worcester Porcelain* 1953*

BEMROSE G. *19th Century English Pottery and Porcelain* 1952*

BIBLIOGRAPHY

BEMROSE W. *Bow, Chelsea, and Derby Porcelain* 1898

BINNS R.W. *Century of Potting in the City of Worcester* 1865; *Worcester China 1852–97* 1897

BINNS W.M. *First Century of English Porcelain* 1906

CHEYNE BOOK OF CHELSEA CHINA AND POTTERY 1924*

CHURCH A.H. *English Porcelain* 1904

COOK C. *Life and Work of Robert Hancock* 1948*

ENGLISH PORCELAIN CIRCLE *Transactions* (Later, English Ceramic Circle) 1928*

FISHER S.W. *English Blue-and-White Porcelain of the 18th Century* 1947*

GILHESPY F.B. *Crown Derby Porcelain* 1951*

HASLEM J. *The Old Derby China Factory* 1876

HAYDEN A. *Spode and His Successors* 1925*

HOBSON R.L. *Catalogue of the English Porcelain in the British Museum* 1905; *Catalogue of the Frank Lloyd Collection of Worcester Porcelain* 1923*; *Worcester Porcelain* 1910*

HODGSON MRS W. *Old English China* 1913

HONEY W.B. *Old English Porcelain* 1928*; *Wedgwood Ware* 1948

HURLBUTT F. *Bow Porcelain* 1926*; *Bristol Porcelain* 1928*; *Chelsea China* 1937; *Old Derby Porcelain* 1925*

JEWITT L. *Ceramic Art of Great Britain* 1878

JOHN W.D. *Nantgarw Porcelain* 1948*

KING W. *Chelsea Porcelain* 1922

LANCASTER H.B. *Liverpool and Her Potters* 1936

MACALISTER MRS D. (Ed) *William Duesbury's London Account Book 1751–53* 1931

MACKENNA F.S. *Champion's Bristol Porcelain* 1947*; *Cookworthy's Plymouth and Bristol Porcelain* 1946*

MAYER J. *History of the Art of Potting in Liverpool* 1855

MEAGER K.S. *Swansea and Nantgarw Potteries* 1949*

MORTON A.E. *Lowestoft China* 1932

NANCE E. MORTON *Pottery and Porcelain of Swansea and Nantgarw* 1942

NIGHTINGALE J.E. *Contributions towards the history of early English Porcelain* 1881

OWEN H. *Two Centuries of Ceramic Art in Bristol* 1873

POUNTNEY W.J. *Old Bristol Potteries* 1920

PRICE E.S. *John Sadler* 1948*

RACKHAM B. *Catalogue of the Herbert Allen Collection of English Porcelain* 1917★; *Catalogue of the Schreiber Collection of English Porcelain* 1928★

SPELMAN W.W.R. *Lowestoft China* 1905

TAPP W.H. *Jefferyes Hamett O'Neale* 1938★

TURNER W. *Transfer Printing on Enamels, Porcelain, and Pottery* 1907

WARD J. *Billingsley and Pardoe* 1896

WORCESTER ROYAL PORCELAIN WORKS MUSEUM *Catalogue of Worcester Porcelain* 1862★

Acknowledgements

I am very conscious of the unavoidable inadequacy of the following section. The inclusion of all the photographs which were made available to me would have raised the price of the book to an unreasonable figure, and several hundreds have had to be put reluctantly to one side. It is hoped that those which remain are sufficiently representative, augmented as they are by the references to the illustrated works of other writers.

Below is a list of those whose material has been used, but it is perhaps well to point out that, as in the case of my own collections, ownership may well have changed hands since the selection was made.

F. A. Barrett, Esq. Figures 3, 8, 15, 37, 38, 52, 61, 62, 92, 94, 109, 135
Charles Woollett & Sons. Figures 1, 47, 63, 78, 132
D. M. & P. Mannheim. Figures 11, 12–14, 123
W. T. Copeland & Sons, Ltd. Frontispiece, Figures 18–20, 53, 54, 83, 84, 100–2, 114, 115, 126
Mrs Dorothy Howell. Figures 23, 66, 116, 137
Delomosne & Son, Ltd. Figures 25, 28, 32–5, 39, 41, 60, 65, 67, 85, 103, 107, 110, 131
F. V. C. de Costa Andrade, Esq. Figures 29–31, 48, 95, 113, 133
Winifred Williams (Antiques). Figures 45, 106, 124, 134
R. L. Kenning, Esq. Figures 51, 55, 97, 136
H. W. Keil, Esq. Figures 56, 57
H. J. Lewis, Esq. Figures 79, 120
Josiah Wedgwood & Sons, Ltd. Figure 86
Cheltenham Museum. Figures 40, 80, 112
Derby Museum. Figures 68, 82
Victoria & Albert Museum. Figures 26, 36, 50, 59, 98, 99, 104, 111, 119, 125
Swansea Museum. Figures 91, 96
British Museum. Figure 105
Worcester Royal Porcelain Co. Ltd. Figure 127
Luton Museum. Figure 130
T. G. Burn, Esq. Figure 10

Description of Illustrations

FRONTISPIECE. SPODE VASE: painted with flowers in natural colours on a gold scale-patterned dark blue ground. *Courtesy of Messrs. W. T. Copeland & Sons Ltd.*

FIGURE 1. WORCESTER MUG. Printed in overglaze black. One of the several 'Milkmaid' designs, outstanding for clarity of engraved line and for technical excellence in every regard.

FIGURE 2. LIVERPOOL CUP AND SAUCER. Printed in underglaze blue. A simple design in the 'Chinese Chippendale' style, intended for quick reproduction on cheaper domestic wares.

FIGURE 3. LIVERPOOL PLATE. Painted in underglaze blue. The economy of line and general arrangement indicate that the decoration was done by one accustomed to painting on the difficult delft surface. A further kinship with the commoner ware is provided by the tin glaze which was used on this specimen.

FIGURE 4. LOWESTOFT JUG. Painted in underglaze blue. The Chinese landscape is particularly detailed, and the 'mask lip' is of an unusually elementary form.

FIGURE 5. WORCESTER BASKET. Painted in underglaze blue. A beautiful design which was probably an exact copy of a Chinese pattern of the famed K'hang H'si period (1662–1722). It seems to have been used almost exclusively for dessert services.

FIGURE 6. LIVERPOOL BOWL. The elementary pink diaper and the heavy style of painting distinguish this design from the more delicate contemporary Worcester ones. The colour scheme is in imitation of the '*famille verte*' palette.

FIGURE 7. LIVERPOOL TEA-POT. An example of the more reticent, well-painted class of Liverpool 'mandarins'.

FIGURE 8. WORCESTER MUG. The obvious anglicization of such designs as this does not detract from the simplicity and colourful charm of the earlier 'mandarins'.

FIGURE 9. WORCESTER COFFEE-POT. The later 'mandarins' are often less carefully painted, even when they are more elaborate, in a style more suited to the decoration of services rather than specimen pieces. The hexagon pattern is perhaps the commonest of all borders, whether in blue or in polychrome, and it is found on the wares of many factories.

FIGURE 10. LONGTON HALL BOWL. Though this provenance is open to some doubt, the photograph is included because of the unusually high quality of the brushwork. The delicate pencilling is allied to washes of blue, brown, and green.

FIGURE 11. BOW LEAF TRAY. The famous 'quail' or 'partridge' pattern, with its usual accompanying floral border in red and gold, is one of the most beautiful of all early English patterns in the Japanese Kakiemon style.

FIGURE 12. REDCLIFF BACKS DISH. A beautiful, well-spaced design from the Bristol factory where the pre-Worcester 'soft paste' body known as 'Lund's Bristol' was made for a short period. It features the Oriental banded hedge which was translated into the familiar 'wheat-sheaf', and the absence of any kind of border is aesthetically good.

FIGURES 13 AND 14. BOW PORCELAIN. Typical examples of peonies, flowering foliage, and stylized rocks, painted in the '*famille rose*' palette of pink, blue, pale mauve, and two shades of green.

FIGURE 15. WORCESTER BOTTLE. This early specimen has the characteristic green predominance of the '*famille verte*' palette, and the jewel-like brilliance of enamel which is a feature of the Worcester painting of the period.

FIGURE 16. WORCESTER (FLIGHTS') DISH. Copies of this early pattern were made at both the later factories. It is known to have been copied from a Chinese '*famille verte*' dish, but the colours are not strictly limited to the Chinese palette.

FIGURE 17. NEW HALL TEA-POT. A pattern in red, blue, and gold, which is well-balanced, and which may well be classed among the later Japans. The shape is typical.

FIGURE 18. SPODE TRAY. A gay pattern which was copied from a much earlier Worcester one, and which is therefore more akin to the Oriental than many other contemporary Spode Japans.

FIGURE 19. SPODE PLATE. English flowers used in a Japanese style, with a foliate and floral border in underglaze blue encircling the central spray. This device is common on the Worcester Japans which influenced this design (Figure 23), and on the Oriental pieces from which Worcester copied.

FIGURE 20. SPODE VASE. Such an amazing combination of Oriental and English motifs is quite alien to the true Japan, though the general appearance and the colours of red, blue, and green, with gilding, give to it an Oriental appearance.

FIGURE 21. SWANSEA PLATE. The natural aversion to hiding their lovely paste prevented the Swansea management from making extensive use of Japan patterns, and accounts for the restraint evident in this rare example. The hachured border is in olive green.

FIGURE 22. WORCESTER DISH. A well-known pattern featuring brocaded diaper and floral rosettes.

FIGURE 23. WORCESTER CUP AND SAUCER. As in the case of the Spode example (Figure 19) the general effect is Oriental, though the flowers are English. Notice the similar underglaze blue border in the centre.

FIGURE 24. WORCESTER (FLIGHTS') PLATE. The delightful painting of this specimen is reminiscent of Japanese Kutani ware. The predominant colours are red and gold, though a good pink and bright greens are used to good effect.

FIGURE 25. WORCESTER JUG. The Chinese landscape is painted in puce, the ground colour is pale yellow, and upon it are Japanese flowers in colour and gilding. The general effect is Oriental, but the arrangement was copied from Meissen, a curious but not uncommon combination of styles.

FIGURE 26. BRISTOL VASE. Apart from the excellence of the modelling, this piece is an object lesson in the daring use of colour. The purple flowers are outstanding on a yellow ground, and the masks and festoons are in natural colours.

FIGURE 27. CHELSEA DISH. The fine painting of fruit and moths on this specimen was done by a painter who afterwards worked at Worcester in the same Meissen style, and who also painted 'exotic birds'.

FIGURE 28. CHELSEA VASE. The flower painting in 'Meissner Blumen' style and the well-proportioned shape of this beautiful piece indicate the Meissen influence.

FIGURE 29. CHELSEA PLATE. This is the sort of decoration which was copied from the engravings in the book written by Philip Miller, the gardener and custodian of the Hans Sloane gardens. The drawing is accurate, and the enamels subdued and true to nature.

FIGURE 30. CHELSEA SUCRIER AND COVER. Another example of the Meissen style, though the photograph cannot show the beauty of the perfected pale yellow ground colour, which has no trace of muddiness in it.

FIGURE 31. CHELSEA DISH. The combination of mazarine blue and burnished gold is splendid in itself, and with the addition of flowers and fruit in natural colours the effect is outstandingly grand. It is known that a decorator named Jenks was responsible for the best gilding of this kind.

FIGURES 32 AND 33. CHELSEA VASES. The fine Chelsea ground colours are seen at their best in conjunction with flower painting in various styles, since flowers are easily adapted to panels of any shape. The ovoid vase has a pale turquoise ground.

FIGURE 34. CHELSEA VASES. Such sets of vases are the height of Chelsea decorative attainment, for though colourful in the extreme the effect is not garish or ostentatious, and the bouquets are detailed and in accurate colour. The ground colour is pale turquoise.

FIGURE 35. CHELSEA PLATES. The simplicity of the Chelsea urn motif and its supporting sprigs contrast effectively with the dark blue border with its floral festoons. The inspiration for this style of decoration was French.

FIGURE 36. COALPORT VASE. The Coalport effort to rival the decoration of the finest Sèvres resulted in pieces of this kind. The treatment of the flowers and foliage, in sprays following the curves of the reserved panel, is particularly effective, as is the gold 'oeil-de-perdrix' pattern on the apple-green ground.

FIGURE 37. COALPORT TRAY. An unusual treatment of flowers, to which the dark blue border is uncommonly subservient for wares of this period.

FIGURE 38. COALPORT PLATE. Among the many artists who painted in the Sèvres style was William Cook. The photograph shows clearly his manner of arranging bouquets in round clusters, though it cannot reveal his peculiar shades of emerald green and bright orange. Green ground colour.

FIGURE 39. DERBY VASES. An important pair of vases representing technical achievement rather than good ceramic art. It is unusual to find such elaboration on pieces made before 1800. 'Marbled' bases.

FIGURES 40 AND 41. DERBY PORCELAIN. The typical Derby shape of the vases is well fitted to panels of flower painting, usually accompanied by scrolled or arabesque gilding. The pair of vases with royal blue ground.

FIGURES 42, 43, AND 44. DERBY PORCELAIN. William Pegg's large flowers and his careful brushwork are shown clearly in these photographs.

FIGURE 45. DERBY PLATE. Similar decoration on Chelsea porcelain is described and illustrated elsewhere, and factors of paste and glaze rather than of decoration lead to an early Derby attribution to this colourful though rather smudged fruit and moth painting.

FIGURE 46. DERBY PLATE. The subject of this illustration lies outside our period, but it is included as being typical of the finest flower painting of the latter years. It was painted by James Rouse. Gold ground.

FIGURES 47 AND 48. LONGTON HALL PORCELAIN. Flower painting on Longton Hall porcelain is usually tentative and immature, but well spaced and pleasingly reticent.

FIGURE 49. NANTGARW PLATES. Small birds or flower sprays were often placed on the rims of Nantgarw plates. These two pieces, with their attractively shaped bouquets, were painted at a London studio.

DESCRIPTION OF ILLUSTRATIONS

FIGURES 50, 51, AND 52. ROCKINGHAM PORCELAIN. Naturalistic flowers in the Derby style, accompanied by ground colours and lavish gilding. Note the 'dotted gold' ground (Figure 51).

FIGURES 53 AND 54. SPODE PORCELAIN. Delicacy of flower painting as a foil to splendid ground colours and gold. Spode colours are gay, but they seldom shout, and one is conscious of technical perfection rather than of ostentation. 'Dotted gold' ground (Figure 53).

FIGURE 55. SWANSEA PLATE. A specimen intended for decoration rather than for use. The fine combination of graceful gilding and an ambitious flower study show to good advantage on the wonderful Swansea/Nantgarw paste.

FIGURES 56 AND 57. SWANSEA PORCELAIN. David Evans was probably a pupil of Billingsley, whose style was also copied by William Pollard, who painted these pieces. The photographs cannot do justice to his delicate colours, but the softness of outline of his bouquets and sprays can be clearly seen.

FIGURE 58. SWANSEA PORCELAIN. It is on record that at Swansea Thomas Baxter was employed to decorate only the most important orders.

FIGURES 59 AND 60. SWANSEA PORCELAIN. Typical styles of flower painting. The sucrier has a turquoise 'oeil de perdrix' ground, the flowers probably by Henry Morris.

FIGURE 61. WORCESTER COFFEE-POT. A most unusual but effective foliate pattern in red and green, quite unlike the usual styles of the period.

FIGURES 62–68. WORCESTER PORCELAIN. A series of illustrations showing the development of Worcester flower painting. Ground colours – yellow (65), apple-green (67), and dark blue (68).

FIGURE 69. WORCESTER (CHAMBERLAINS') PLATE. A lovely example of the perfected use of naturalistic flower painting, matt cobalt ground colour, and raised gilding.

FIGURES 70–73. WORCESTER (CHAMBERLAINS') PORCELAIN. The botanical style of an unknown artist is clearly seen in these photographs. The use of flat gilding on the lovely Chamberlain peach ground (Figure 71) illustrates the factory penchant for borders of the Worcestershire oak-leaf and acorn. The large figure (72) has a mazarine border.

FIGURE 74. WORCESTER (CHAMBERLAINS') VASES. The reverse sides are decorated with elaborate, carefully drawn gilt scroll work. Mazarine ground, the fruit probably by Steele.

FIGURE 75. WORCESTER (GRAINGERS') BASKET. A clever and effective use of gold seaweed pattern with a pink rose thrown carelessly upon it.

FIGURE 76. WORCESTER (CHAMBERLAINS') DISH. The pure white 'Regent' paste, moulded in low relief, is an effective background for a simple botanical flower spray in blue and green.

FIGURE 77. WORCESTER (CHAMBERLAINS') BASKET. The shells are painted in their natural colours on a pale salmon-pink ground enriched with flat gold flower sprays, and the bouquet of naturalistic flowers is painted on the white. The effect is colourful yet restrained, dainty, and not overburdened.

FIGURE 78. CHELSEA TEA-POT. An example of painting of the 'purple landskip' class of the Catalogues, and of course a translation of a Meissen style.

FIGURE 79. COALPORT VASE. Topographical views form the greater proportion of the Coalport landscapes; this one is subsidiary to characteristic Coalbrookdale applied flowers, painted in natural colours.

FIGURE 80. DAVENPORT TRAY. Many pieces of this sort, bearing pictures of the Cotswold spa, were produced by Davenports and by the two main Worcester factories, probably to special order. The ground colour of this specimen is particularly good, in a pleasing tone of cobalt blue.

FIGURE 81. DERBY DISH. Typical Derby landscape painting, possibly by Boreman, with a border of 'Smith's Blue'.

FIGURE 82. ROCKINGHAM PLATE. A river scene rendered in minute detail, accompanied by elaborate gilding on an even grey ground colour of good quality.

FIGURE 83. SPODE PLATE. No finer landscape has ever been painted on porcelain, and this specimen was an exhibit at the 1851 Exhibition. The gold trellissed border is a masterpiece of accurate drawing, fine blue colour, and perfected mercury gilding.

FIGURE 84. SPODE PLATE. A beautiful style of English landscape painting, in the 'oil painting' manner. Buff border.

FIGURE 85. SWANSEA PLATE. A harbour scene painted in a manner reminiscent of much Marseilles faïence of the 1770–80 period, but with the characteristic roses and 'dotted gold' ground of the Swansea factory.

FIGURE 86. WEDGWOOD PORCELAIN. The porcelain made between 1805 and about 1815 seldom bears outstanding decoration. John Cutts purchased the Pinxton factory in 1804, and was later employed at Etruria, probably between 1812 and 1815, at which time he was responsible for careless but fresh-looking landscape painting of this kind. Each scene is named.

FIGURE 87. WORCESTER (FLIGHTS') DISH. From a service painted with views of the Welsh border country, by an artist whose grey tones impart a wintry effect which is exaggerated by the unmistakable cold quality of the Flights apple-green ground colour.

FIGURE 88. WORCESTER (CHAMBERLAINS') PLATE. The painting of this Irish landscape was done by Robert Brewer in his typical Derby style, and the accompanying gilt border might well have been done at the same factory.

FIGURE 89. WORCESTER (CHAMBERLAINS') SAUCER. Humphrey Chamberlain painted good landscapes as backgrounds to his figure subjects. The 'pebbled' salmon-pink ground is characteristic.

FIGURE 90. WORCESTER (CHAMBERLAINS') MUG. This is 'architectural' painting, with the dark claret ground which was usually enriched with gilt foliate sprays springing from the rococo reserve.

FIGURE 91. SWANSEA ICE-PAIL. Reserved as the last illustration in this section is a fine example of landscape painting at its best. There is documentary evidence to show that Thomas Baxter was responsible for the work upon the large service to which this well-shaped specimen belongs.

FIGURE 92. BOW PLATE. Painted with the brightly-coloured 'agitated' exotic bird by a Giles artist whose style may be seen on the wares of several factories.

FIGURE 93. CHELSEA MUG. The early Chelsea naturalistic birds are full of movement and colour.

FIGURE 94. CHELSEA DISH. The 'plump' exotic birds described in the text, as painted here with no ground colour or border pattern, are probably the most decorative of all the various types.

FIGURE 95. CHELSEA VASE. The 'transitional' birds form the connecting link between the 'naturalistic' and the 'exotic'. This lovely example features the characteristic use of mazarine and burnished gold.

FIGURE 96. LONGTON HALL TEA-POT. An early attempt by the factory artists in the style later perfected at Worcester. It is rare to find a scale ground on wares from this small factory.

FIGURE 97. MADELEY VASE. T. Martin Randall's imitation of Sèvres porcelain was well-nigh perfect, and his exotic bird painting second to none.

FIGURE 98. MINTON SHELL DISH. Painted in Sèvres style, with a fine turquoise border.

FIGURE 99. NANTGARW PLATE. From the Mackintosh service, of which each piece is painted with a different bird. As in the case of most Nantgarw porcelain, the decoration was done in London.

FIGURE 100. SPODE DISH. A well-known Spode pattern, with well-painted birds in natural surroundings, feathers, and white flowers raised upon a rather dull lavender ground which needs to be viewed by candle-light.

FIGURE 101. SPODE PLATE. An example of a style of decoration designed to provide replacements for a service made at another factory, in this particular case, at Chelsea.

FIGURE 102. SPODE PATTERN BOOK. The pages of this prized possession of the modern Copeland factory are opened at the design used for the plate featured in the previous illustration. This, and every other in the book, was most beautifully rendered in water-colour.

FIGURES 103–107. WORCESTER PORCELAIN. Exotic birds in various styles.

FIGURE 108. WORCESTER (CHAMBERLAINS') PASTILLE BURNER. A revival of the earlier style, painted in a reserve with matt and burnished gold scrolled border, on a matt cobalt-blue ground.

FIGURE 109. DERBY VASE. An early style of figure painting, very crudely drawn, and seemingly an afterthought to the brightly coloured applied flowers which form the main decoration.

FIGURE 110. DERBY VASE. A very fine example of the inimitable painting of cupids by Richard Askew.

FIGURE 111. MINTON BOWL. Imitation of Sèvres porcelain reached its climax about 1850, when a number of French workmen were engaged as potters and decorators. Among them, Carl Henk is well known for his figure painting in this particular style.

FIGURE 112. MINTON VASE. The *pâte-sur-pâte* technique introduced from Sèvres by M. L. Solon falls outside our period, but this example of it is included as a matter of interest.

FIGURE 113. PLYMOUTH BEAKER. The freshness of the colours of this little panel of figure painting, to say nothing of its humour, make it a very pleasant and refreshing piece of ceramic decoration.

FIGURES 114 AND 115. SPODE PORCELAIN. The outstanding features of Spode figure painting are vividness of colour and accomplished drawing.

FIGURES 116 AND 117. WORCESTER (FLIGHTS') PORCELAIN. Two styles of monochrome painting by James Pennington. The border of the plate (which is from a service made for the Duke of Clarence in 1792), is a marvel of accurate drawing and accomplished mercury gilding.

FIGURE 118. WORCESTER (CHAMBERLAINS') PLATE. Faults may often be found in Humphrey Chamberlain's draughtsmanship, but there can be no doubt about his expert brushwork and fine choice of colour. This specimen is from a service made to the order of George IV (as Prince Regent) for presentation to the King of Hanover, and the painting represents a scene from 'Paradise Lost'.

FIGURE 119. WORCESTER (FLIGHTS') VASES. Figure painting was not the least of Thomas Baxter's attainments, as this illustration shows. Note the 'jewelled' borders copied from Sèvres.

FIGURES 120 AND 121. WORCESTER (CHAMBERLAINS') JUGS. Jugs of this sort were often made in sets. Note the oak-leaf and acorn motif of the border on what was a presentation jug (since the names and dates of birth of the twin recipients are inscribed under the base, and their initials in gold are on the sides), and that the Dr Syntax picture is an exact reproduction of the Rowlandson print in the 1812 edition of *The Tour of Dr Syntax in Search of the Picturesque*.

FIGURE 122. WORCESTER (GRAINGERS') VASE. It is tempting to credit the classical painting to Baxter, though it is not known that he worked at the factory. It should be noted that Graingers' decoration, in whatever style, was invariably of the highest quality.

FIGURE 123. BOW PLATE. The addition of the coat of arms to the typical Kakiemon decoration of this specimen in no way detracts from its restrained beauty.

FIGURES 124 AND 125. BRISTOL PORCELAIN. Examples of cups and saucers from services made for special presentation. Daniel Ludlow of Camden (124) and Sir Robert Smyth (125).

FIGURE 126. SPODE PLATE. Spode 'armorial china' is invariably tasteful and seldom overcrowded with decoration, in spite of the inevitable colourfulness of the heraldry. The ground colour of this piece is pale apple-green.

FIGURE 127. WORCESTER PLATE. An armorial plate of the Wall period, notable for enamel colours of good quality, a border of intense mazarine blue, and a restrained, graceful pattern drawn thereupon in soft honey gilding.

FIGURES 128 AND 129. WORCESTER (CHAMBERLAINS') PLATES. These illustrations show the factory's inimitable use of heraldry, fine ground colours, and good mercury gilding, particularly on the lovely piece (Figure 128) painted in miniature style by Plant, which has no less than seven gold border patterns. The use of contrasting tones of gold, some matt and some burnished, and all intricately tooled, is visible even in the photograph. The ground colours of the two pieces are matt cobalt and claret respectively.

FIGURE 130. CAUGHLEY SUCRIER AND COVER. Particulars of the career and work of Fidelle Duvivier will be found in the text. He painted at various factories, and this example of his work, probably at Caughley, is far above the average low standard of Salopian decoration.

FIGURES 131 AND 132. CHELSEA PLATES. The lifelike appearance and vitality of O'Neale's animal painting is clearly apparent in these early specimens.

FIGURE 133. CHELSEA DISH. The fable painting of Jefferyes Hamett O'Neale, with flowers probably added by another hand.

FIGURE 134. CHELSEA BOWL. A beautiful painting by William Duvivier, the founder of a school of painting best known through the work of O'Neale.

FIGURE 135. CHELSEA MUGS. The Sèvres style is very evident in these dainty specimens, with typically chubby children painted by John Donaldson. The painted panels are reserved on a mazarine ground, vermiculated in gold.

FIGURE 136. DERBY CUP. This enlargement provides an interesting study of Fidelle Duvivier's brushwork, particularly with regard to his remarkable strength and clarity of essential line.

FIGURE 137. WORCESTER TEA-POY AND COVER. Hancock's transfer prints take to themselves quite a different appearance by reason of the enamels and gilding which were added to them at Giles' London studio.

I WORCESTER MUG: about 1765

2 LIVERPOOL CUP and SAUCER: about 1775

3 LIVERPOOL PLATE: about 1765

4 LOWESTOFT JUG: about 1760

129

5 WORCESTER BASKET: about 1760

6 LIVERPOOL BOWL: about 1760

130

7 LIVERPOOL TEA-POT: about 1760   8 WORCESTER MUG: about 1760

9 WORCESTER COFFEE-POT: about 1765

10 LONGTON HALL BOWL: about 1760

11 BOW LEAF TRAY: about 1755

12 REDCLIFF BACKS (or LUND'S BRISTOL) DISH: about 1755

13 BOW BOWL: about 1760

14 BOW MUG: about 1760

15 WORCESTER BOTTLE: about 1752–5

16 FLIGHTS' WORCESTER DISH: about 1790

17 NEW HALL TEA-POT: about 1790

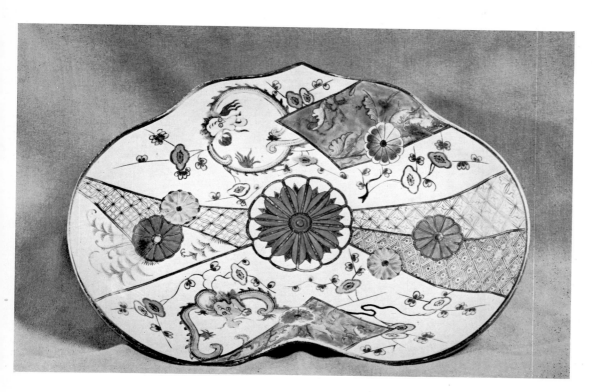

18 SPODE TRAY: about 1795

19 SPODE PLATE: about 1810

20 SPODE VASE: about 1805

21 SWANSEA PLATE: about 1815

22 WORCESTER DISH: about 1770

23 WORCESTER CUP and SAUCER:
about 1765

24 FLIGHTS' WORCESTER PLATE:
about 1810

25 WORCESTER JUG: about 1765

26 BRISTOL VASE: about 1770

27 CHELSEA DISH: about 1755

28 CHELSEA VASE: about 1755

29 CHELSEA PLATE: about 1755–60

30 CHELSEA SUCRIER and COVER: about 1760

31 CHELSEA DISH: about 1760

32 & 33 CHELSEA VASES: about 1760-5

34 CHELSEA VASES: about 1765

35 CHELSEA PLATES: about 1765

36 COALPORT VASE: about 1850

37 COALPORT TRAY: about 1840

38 COALPORT PLATE: about 1840

39 DERBY VASES: about 1790

40 DERBY PORCELAIN: about 1790

41 DERBY VASES: about 1800

42 DERBY PLATE: about 1820

43 DERBY TRAY: about 1820

44 DERBY PLATE: about 1820

45 DERBY PLATE: about 1755

46 DERBY PLATE: about 1880

47 LONGTON HALL BOWL: about 1755

48 LONGTON HALL SAUCE-BOAT: about 1755

49 NANTGARW PLATES: about 1815

50 ROCKINGHAM VASE: about 1830

51 ROCKINGHAM VASE: about 1830

52 ROCKINGHAM
PLATE:
about 1830

53 SPODE FRUIT STAND: about 1820

54 SPODE VASE: about 1810

55 & 56 SWANSEA PLATES: about 1815

57 SWANSEA PLATES: about 1815

58 SWANSEA PORCELAIN: about 1815

59 SWANSEA SUCRIER and COVER: about 1815

60 SWANSEA VASE: about 1815   61 WORCESTER COFFEE-POT: about 1755

62 WORCESTER DISH: about 1760

63 WORCESTER BASKETS: about 1785

64 WORCESTER TEA-POT: about 1765

65 WORCESTER CROCUS POTS: about 1770

66 WORCESTER CUP and SAUCER: about 1770

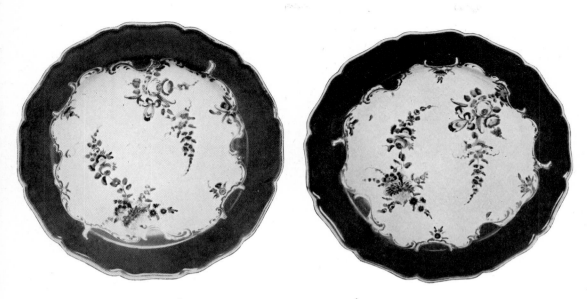

67 WORCESTER PLATES: about 1775

68 WORCESTER PLATE: about 1785

69 CHAMBERLAINS' WORCESTER PLATE: about 1810

70 CHAMBERLAINS' WORCESTER CUP and SAUCER: about 1815

71 CHAMBERLAINS' WORCESTER PLATE: about 1815

72 CHAMBERLAINS' WORCESTER PLATE: about 1815

73 CHAMBERLAINS' WORCESTER SPILL-VASE: about 1815

164

74 CHAMBERLAINS' WORCESTER VASES: about 1820

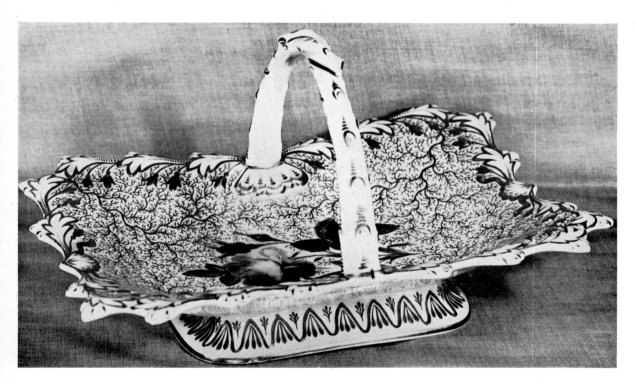

75 GRAINGERS' WORCESTER BASKET: about 1830

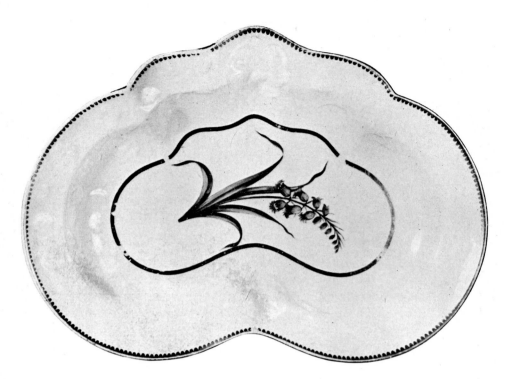

76 CHAMBERLAINS' WORCESTER DISH: about 1830

77 CHAMBERLAINS' WORCESTER BASKET: about 1830

78 CHELSEA TEA-POT: about 1755

79 COALPORT VASE: about 1830

80 DAVENPORT TRAY: about 1850

81 DERBY DISH: about 1785

82 ROCKINGHAM PLATE: about 1830

83 SPODE PLATE: about 1850

84 SPODE PLATE: about 1845

85 SWANSEA PLATE: about 1815

86 WEDGWOOD PORCELAIN: about 1815

87 FLIGHTS' WORCESTER DISH: about 1810

88 CHAMBERLAINS' WORCESTER PLATE: about 1790

89 CHAMBERLAINS' WORCESTER SAUCER: about 1815

90 CHAMBERLAINS' WORCESTER MUG: about 1820

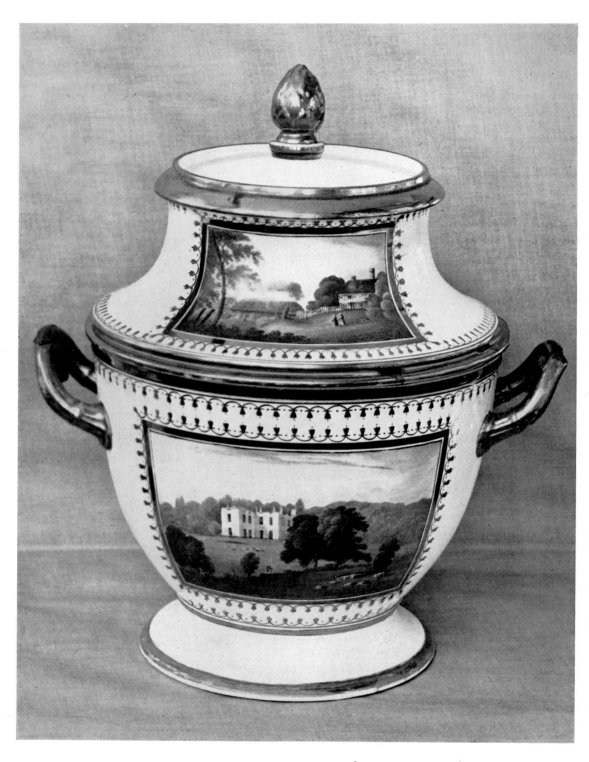

91 SWANSEA ICE-PAIL: about 1820

176

92 BOW PLATE: about 1770

93 CHELSEA MUG: about 1760

94 CHELSEA DISH: about 1760

95 CHELSEA VASE: about 1760

96 LONGTON HALL TEA-POT: about 1755

97 MADELEY VASE: about 1830–40

98 MINTON DISH: about 1825

99 NANTGARW PLATE: about 1820

100 SPODE DISH: about 1800

101 SPODE PLATE: date unknown

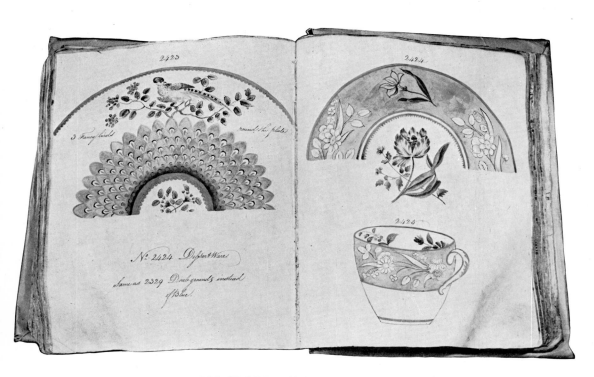

102 SPODE PATTERN BOOK

103 WORCESTER
TEA-POT:
about 1770

104 WORCESTER DISH: about 1770

105 WORCESTER VASE: about 1770

106 WORCESTER DISH: about 1770

107 WORCESTER PLATE: about 1775

108 CHAMBERLAINS' WORCESTER
PASTILLE-BURNER: about 1830

109 DERBY VASE: about 1755

110 DERBY VASE: about 1770

III MINTON BOWL: about 1850-60

112 MINTON VASE: about 1875

113 PLYMOUTH BEAKER:
about 1768-70

114 SPODE BOWL: about 1815

115 SPODE VASE: about 1822

116 FLIGHTS' WORCESTER JUG: about 1800

189

117 FLIGHTS' WORCESTER PLATE 1792

118 CHAMBERLAINS' WORCESTER PLATE: about 1815

119 FLIGHTS' WORCESTER VASES: about 1815

120 & 121 CHAMBERLAINS' WORCESTER JUGS: about 1830

122 GRAINGERS' WORCESTER VASE: about 1820

123 BOW PLATE: about 1765

124 BRISTOL SUCRIER and DISH: about 1775

125 BRISTOL CUP and SAUCER 1776

126 SPODE PLATE: about 1810

127 WORCESTER PLATE: about 1770

128 CHAMBERLAINS' WORCESTER PLATE: about 1820

129 CHAMBERLAINS' WORCESTER PLATE: about 1845

130 CAUGHLEY SUCRIER: about 1773

197

131 CHELSEA PLATES: about 1750

132 CHELSEA PLATES: about 1750

133 CHELSEA DISH: about 1755

134 CHELSEA BOWL: about 1752

135 CHELSEA MUGS:
about 1760–5

136 DERBY CUP: about 1770

137 WORCESTER TEAPOY: about 1765

Index

Plate references are printed in bolder type.